GET FRESH
with Glynn Christian

More Cookery from Pebble Mill at One

Glynn Christian

D0718265

BRITISH BROADCASTING CORPORATION

Acknowledgements

Getting fresh with new fruits and vegetables, meats and fish, was also a good opportunity for me to get aquainted with some of the new equipment available for the kitchen.

Amongst the items I found most useful – and those who saw my television programmes will have seen them demonstrated – were The Magimix Food Processor, Convectionaire Oven, Egea pasta-making machine, Altea ravioli trays, a wooden knife-block, and the mandatory, non-absorbent white chopping boards. Information about all these is available from Divertimenti, 68 Marylebone Lane, W1 or The French Kitchen Shop, Westbourne Grove, London W2.

I also tested the see-through range of saucepans and casseroles called Vision by Corning Glass and new, brass-bound knives by Wilkinson Sword.

Generous support was given by suppliers of *Get Fresh* produce. I was helped a lot by The Fresh Fruit and Vegetable Bureau and Mr Gerry Newey of Walsall. Equally bountiful were The New Zealand Lamb Information Bureau, The New Zealand Kiwi Fruit Information Bureau, the Dutch Meat Bureau, the Dutch Vegetable Growers, Marine Harvest of Edinburgh (salmon), Silver Trout Limited, Romsey, and, especially, Marika Hanbury Tenison and The Sea Fish Industry Authority.

Of course, most encouragement comes from those who buy books or who wrote in to Pebble Mill's office. I'm most grateful for that, for the encouragement of those in BBC Publications, for the generosity of the presenters of Pebble Mill at One, and for the talents of the photographers, Paul Kemp and Laurie Sparham, who worked on the book's jacket.

Published by the
British Broadcasting Corporation
35 Marylebone High Street
London W1M 4AA

ISBN 0 563 20108 8
First published 1982
© Glynn Christian 1982

Typeset by Phoenix Photosetting, Chatham
Printed in England
by Mackays of Chatham

CONTENTS

Note: The metric recipes in this book are not translations of the imperial weights and measures but are alternative metric recipes. As the recipes are not equivalent to each other it is important not to combine measurements from imperial and metric recipes.

INTRODUCTION

Don't be misled. This is not a book of 150 new ways with salads. It is a fresh look at what is happening in our food shops today. It introduces much that is new, reminds you of some old favourites you might have forgotten – and tells you what to do with them both, mainly with original recipes and tips.

Since the enormous increase in overseas travel that began with the introduction of the inclusive holiday in the late 60s, food in the United Kingdom has changed out of all recognition. When you speak of British food these days you must include Chinese and Indian takeaway, pizzas, kebabs and hamburgers. Indeed there are thousands of children who know more about foreign food than the food of their fathers, yet have never left these shores.

The demand created by travellers, the exciting leavening introduced by our immigrant communities, and the excellent job done by the media's creative and responsible food writers have stimulated the marketing organisations. There has never been such a wide variety of food available to the consumer. Of course, this does not mean such a choice is uniformly available throughout the country. But slowly even the supermarkets are listening to demand and offering wider ranges of herbs and spices, new and different fruits and vegetables, better ranges of tea and coffee. Noticeably more are opening or extending delicatessen counters where you can find real, farmhouse cheeses, and sausages from all over Europe. It goes some way to soften the blow of the disappearance of the corner shops.

Yet what use is this new variety if there is no one to tell the customer how he or she can benefit? That is precisely why my Get Fresh programmes and book were planned, and I hope they succeed in taking away some of the mystery from a few of the more weird and wonderful items you've noticed recently. Once you know about them they can make cooking and eating a great deal more fun for everyone.

The biggest changes we can all see are in the green-grocers. Many vegetables we used to think of as foreign and expensive are now part of the English grown crop – courgettes, aubergines and red peppers, for instance. That means they are cheaper and available for much longer, and no longer such a specialty. Wondrous tropical fruits like the mango, lime and kiwi fruit are already becoming commonplace in many towns and cities and soon will be as much part of our diet as the avocado has become. Remember, only fifteen years ago the avocado itself was still a rare and wonderful treat.

Fish buying is changing, partly through the new techniques which allow trout and salmon in particular to be farmed, which has brought prices down dramatically. New cuts of lamb have been developed for the busier housewife. Pieces of bacon – bacon joints – are soon going to be far more common, in the same way that turkey has recently become part of our normal diet rather than being relegated to holidays.

Once I began to open my mind to the exciting possibilities offered by these new opportunities and flavours I also began thinking of cooking techniques which, although foreign to us, are commonplace in other countries. Thus, the series includes instructions on making your own pasta, how to make the see-through pastry for a proper apple strudel, how to bone fish, butterfly a leg of lamb, pickle salmon. You'll also find fresh new ideas for things you thought you knew all about – a cake flavoured with tea, a soufflé thickened with chocolate, parsnips made into a pâté . . . even how to paint pastry in imitation of medieval banquet food.

Certainly you will find some of the ingredients I have introduced a little difficult to find. And others will be expensive, at least for the time being. But there is always a good reason why they have been chosen. That pickled salmon, for instance, tastes better than smoked salmon but will cost less than half the price. Fruit on

Toast is a simple way to enjoy special fruit that are not quite ripe. The sorbet and ice cream recipes tell you how to avoid these melting too quickly when they are served.

Although I very much emphasise the use of fresh fruit, vegetables, meat and fish, you will find I have used the occasional tinned product, for some are exceptionally good. Most noticeable is my use of tinned plum tomatoes for sauces and as a cooking medium. I have a special reason for using it so much in this book. I wish to help convince the great British palate that it has been misled about tomatoes – those orange orbs sold as 'rock hard and proud of it' are not tomatoes at all. Real tomatoes are red, rugged, solid-fleshed, and bursting with a sweetness and flavour that is exciting and rewarding. Slowly growers are introducing such tomatoes back on to this market, from Morocco in the first place, but now from elsewhere; they are usually called 'beefsteak' or 'marmonde'. Until they are accepted as the basic tomato in this country I shall push more and more the use of tinned tomatoes, simply so you know what tomatoes *should* taste like. When you do, and when you can buy them, I shall use fresh tomatoes.

My hope is that this book will stimulate you to take a fresh look at what is in your shops, encouraging you to have the confidence to go out and buy or try something new, and to experiment with my recipes, adding or subtracting as you think best, to make your own creations.

The choice in our shops has never been better, but unless we make use of it, there is every likelihood it will be taken away from us. How often have we heard a shopkeeper saying; 'There isn't the demand'. *You* be the demand, and make that demand heard. Then you'll be able to get fresh with whoever you like . . . whenever you like.

SOME NEW INGREDIENTS...

The New Fruits

Avocado: one variety or another is available all year round now. Flavours vary little, whether the skin is wrinkled or smooth, green or black. Oil and vinegar dressing plus prawns is the most popular way of serving avocado, but I can't imagine why, as both main ingredients are so bland. Use sliced avocado bathed in lemon juice as a salad ingredient or as an attractive substitute for rice as the base for hot or cold chicken or fish dishes. When making a mousse or soup, always include the bright green lining just inside the skin.

Feijoa: still rather rare, this is egg-shaped and a pale pastel green. The flesh is white and slightly grainy with soft seeds. It is extremely aromatic and just a half, sliced over ice cream, is quite an experience.

Kiwi Fruit: shaped like a furry brown egg, one kiwi fruit has twice as much vitamin C as an orange. Simply cut in half and scoop out all the flesh, as though eating an egg. Used mainly as a decoration because of its bright green colour but a good substitute for avocado in a seafood salad or in summer salads, too. Actually has little real flavour when soft-ripe so use it when firm and always sprinkle with lime, orange or lemon juice or with a liqueur, especially in fruit salads. Do not follow any recipe which suggests making a purée, as this crushes the black seeds, making a terribly bitter flavour.

Kumquats: these tiny pungent relatives of the orange are eaten skin and all. Slice them into fruit salads or into a sauce for roasted duck. Or cook them gently in syrup to spoon over ice cream, to serve with strawberries and other soft fruit.

Lime: possibly the most important and simplest addition to your repertoire of ingredients, this small, vivid-green citrus has a sweet/sour flavour like nothing else. On fish and with fruit it adds an unmistakeable touch of the tropics, and once you are confident with it, can be used where ever you would use lemon or orange. The grated green skin is a good garnish or flavouring in mayonnaise and sauces. *But* beware – there is also something else called a Florida lime or lemon lime, and even these come in various guises. Both imposters have the same bright green, smooth skin; one looks like a lime, the other like a lemon. Inside both have yellow flesh and taste like a lemon, being, in fact, the *citron vert* we normally only see in dried peel at Christmas time. Attractive though they are, they will only give you the flavour of lemon and thus are a waste of money. Once you know the flavour of lime, you can tell a real one simple by slightly scratching the skin – the imposters will smell of lemon. If you are not certain – and most shopkeepers simply do not know that Florida and lemon limes are not proper limes – then ask to see the box in which they came. If you still make a mistake, then take some of the offending citrus back to the shop and point out the flavour difference to the manager; if he's worthwhile, he will thank you for telling him something he didn't know. These mock limes are more likely to be seen in the first few dismal months of the year, when I am desperate for a taste of the tropics. Very irritating.

Lychees: recognisable by their rather knobbly round, red shells, fresh lychees are amongst the most delicious of snack fruits. Crack the shells over a bowl, so you catch the juice, then cut out the black stone. Very good as a palate freshener during a rich Christmas lunch. I marinate them with segments of tangerine in a little vodka and a sprinkle of rosewater, and give everyone a tiny, cold helping while they are waiting for the pudding.

Mango: soon this will be as common as the avocado has become. They should be firm but yield slightly to the pressure of your hand when you hold them in your palm, and they must always have an intoxicating perfume. Very soft mangoes are excellent for making into purées for fools, ice creams or sorbets. The best accompaniments are lime and orange juice, or black rum in almost any proportion. Other sweet fruits mix well – soft fruits, passion fruit and lychees especially. Used sliced with cold chicken, chopped into a rice salad, in a green salad to accompany ham or turkey. Or soak in a little orange liqueur in a long glass then top with a Spanish 'methode champenoise' sparkling wine.

Passion Fruit: purple in colour, like a slightly flattened egg and either quite smooth or very wrinkled. A wrinkled one should never smell acidic for this means it is so old the interior has begun to ferment. The interior is actually lots of black seeds in a fragrant orange pulp. You eat it all, but some strain out the seeds. Silly. Passion fruit has no peer as the finishing touch to a fruit salad or *any* dish of tropical fruit. One passion fruit per helping stirred into a fruit salad, or dribbled over mango, banana, peaches, strawberries or papaya is perfectly wonderful. If you can get hold of plenty, the proper way to eat them is simply to bite the top off and squirt the pulp straight into your mouth. This can change your life.

Pawpaw/papaya: the names are interchangeable and there are many types of each, all of which taste quite similar and so it doesn't matter what you call them. Ranging from golden-yellow to green on the outside and from golden-yellow to an almost watermelon pink (my favourite) inside, these fruits are quite ovoid at the bottom but stretch up into a more cylindrical shape. They can weigh up to several pounds each. The texture should be similar to that of a mango but less juicy and the peach-plus flavour is also less pronounced, but nonetheless attractive and tropical. Slice a pawpaw or papaya in half lengthwise, scoop out the seeds, which look like kingsize caviar, sprinkle the flesh with lime or lemon juice and enjoy, especially for breakfast. Fabulous addition to fruit salads, of course.

Physallis: once known as the cape gooseberry or as the golden berry, this berry seems to be making a comeback. It is an intensely flavoured, golden berry in a brown 'chinese-lantern' casing. Eaten raw, its perfumed sweet/sourness is addictive and goes as well with pâtés as with ice creams. Especially good with ginger, and an interesting addition to apple or pear crumbles and so on. Well worth trying.

Pomegranate: these have always seemed exotic to me, but in reality I don't find they have much to offer. You can cut them in half and eat all the interior seeds, pulp and juice. Or extract the juice using a lemon squeezer, sweeten and use as a sauce or flavouring, for this is a simple grenadine. Pomegranate syrup can be bought in many eastern shops.

Plantain: although a type of banana, one which grows downwards rather than up, this is used mainly as a vegetable as it must be cooked. When baked whole or deep fried as chips or in slices, it usually turns a nice bright yellow colour but still tastes rather starchy, as indeed it is.

Sharon Fruit: when these were known as persimmons you couldn't eat them until they were really soft and the inside had turned into a pulp. New varieties from Israel have solved that problem, and sharon fruit are now sweet and tasty at any time. Tasting of honey, they are delightful when simply scooped from a fruit that has been cut in half.

Tamarillo: another name change, at least for me. These were always called tree tomatoes in New Zealand but have reverted to their original name now they are being exported. For my money they are even more exciting than kiwi fruit with a truly gorgeous dark red skin; shaped like a pointed egg, the tamarillo is packed with a golden sweet/sour flesh and red/black seeds. Wonderful eaten like an egg, scooped out with added sugar. But can also be grilled to serve with savoury food, cooked gently in syrup for pudding, made into stunning sorbets or ice creams, sauce . . . almost anything. And the added reward is the magnificent ruby colour the seeds impart to such puddings.

The New Vegetables

Artichoke: there are two types. Best known is the so-called globe artichoke, a green sphere of small green leaves. The simplest way to cook one is to cut off the stalk, rub the wound with lemon, then immediately cook in masses of boiling water which is slightly acidulated for 40 minutes. Drain then serve with melted butter, perhaps flavoured with garlic. Pick off the leaves and prise off the fleshy pad at the base of each between your teeth. When you reach the artichoke's middle, scoop away the hairy choke then enjoy the delicious cup of flesh underneath – known as the *fond*. If you want to serve the artichoke cold, serve with a vinaigrette rather than butter. You can also cut an artichoke in half, horizontally (this would be thrown away anyway) and excavate the choke before cooking. Use masses of lemon juice to prevent the fast discolouration that is always imminent. Cook for only 20 minutes and serve with the sauce, hot or cold, actually in the artichoke. The Jerusalem artichoke is a knobbly, earthy root vegetable that is hell to peel. It is at its best cooked in milk and butter before being puréed to make a soup often called Palestine soup.

Aubergine: also known as egg plant, for although aubergines are now usually a glossy purple colour the white variety was once better known. They are almost always cooked with their skin intact, and should be sliced and sprinkled with salt and allowed to drain for an hour or two, which gets rid of some of the intrinsic bitterness. Aubergines are terrific fried in thick slices, but absorb a phenomenal amount of oil, becoming velvety smooth and delicious as they do; olive oil is best of all. Aubergines are used for the lining of the best known of the Greek dishes called moussaka and are vital to such Mediterranean vegetable dishes as ratatouille.

Bean sprouts: these can be the sprouts of many a type of seed or bean, alfalfa or mung beans being perhaps the best known. Better for you and less bitter if there is no green to be seen. Eat them raw in salads, or toss them in butter with garlic as an interesting hot vegetable.

Celeriac: ugly and knobbly and also called celery root, celeriac is one of the most exciting and versatile additions you can make to your vegetable repertoire. It has a definite celery-like taste. Finely grated raw celeriac with a good dressing is a most refreshing salad. Cooked and puréed with butter, garlic and parsley it is a clean-tasting, non-stodgy alternative to potato, and very good with winter foods, particularly game. It can also be used *with* potato – cook celeriac in small cubes then add it to creamy mashed potatoes at the last minute.

Chilli peppers: some are thin and long, some are short and fat. A general rule is the smaller they are, the hotter they are. You only need one or two to flavour a sauce for 4 people, but always remove the seeds first for this is where the most fiery effect is to be found.

Chinese leaves: a great market success without the benefit of much help from the media. Chinese leaves, also called chinese cabbage, look like a rather pallid but tightly packed cos lettuce. They may be sliced finely for salad but have a strange bitter flavour disliked by many, including me. It is popular cooked too, in which case blanch it quickly in boiling water first, as this will reduce the bitter flavour. Then cook in some stock or in butter. It keeps its green colour better than many other green vegetables. It is a popular addition to stir-fried chinese dishes and for this you can either blanch or not blanch first as you choose.

Coriander: flat leaved and green, rather like flat leaf parsley (petroushka), coriander has a strange bitter flavour
which is essential to much Middle Eastern, Thai and
Mexican food. Use very sparingly at first with recipes
that specifically call for it – experiment later. Coriander
seed comes from the same source but has a sweet,
orange-like flavour that bears no resemblance to that of
the leaf.

Courgettes: still called by their Italian name, zucchini, in
some countries. Properly a specially bred miniature
marrow, but sometimes you buy baby marrows. Both
taste the same. Because they are now part of the estab-
lished English crop they are widely available for long
periods and quite cheap. The usual way to present them
is to wash them and slice them in long diagonal thick
pieces. You can sprinkle them with salt and let them
drain of their slight bitterness – or not as the fancy takes
you. The drained courgettes may be squeezed in the
hands to dry them thoroughly and then chopped. The
resultant mush may be used as the basis of an elegant
stuffing, especially when mixed with cream cheese and
egg and herbs. Or the slices can be seethed in butter,
deep fried in or out of batter. They make lots of extra
liquid during cooking if they have not first been
drained. Courgettes marry well with most herbs but
have a special affinity with tarragon.

Fennel: you recognise this easily as it looks like a pearly
white, flattened onion with no skin and has green fronds
on top. It has a lovely liquorice-like flavour and can be
sliced finely raw for use in salads or cut in half and
braised to make a sensational hot dish. Otherwise cut it
in thin slices and poach in a mixture of oil and lemon
juice with garlic and herbs and serve cold in that same
juice, as a starter.

Garlic: now don't be silly, garlic is not only very good
for you, but is perfectly delicious – you've probably
eaten it dozens of times without knowing, especially if

you like Chinese or Indian food. In early summer look for the big fresh bulbs; the cloves of these are juicy and less strong than the older, dried ones and are very good sliced finely over tomato salad. Otherwise peel, finely chop or squeeze garlic through a garlic press. An excellent way of controlling the amount of garlic in a dish is to add the whole cloves, skin and all. The flavour will permeate, but those who really like the stuff can pop open the cloves and eat the whole thing – garlic like this becomes almost creamy. Eating parsley will avoid breath problems short term. If you have eaten so much you are a hazard the next day, then the solution is to bathe and to wash your hair. Garlic is exuded through the skin, taking impurities with it – unless you bathe you will smell of garlic no matter what you do to your breath.

Green ginger: the root of the ginger plant is extraordinarily versatile, adding a bite and exotic flavour to fish (especially), poultry, meat, fruit and vegetables. It is the mad, rugged pale brown root with knobs and a smooth shiny creamy brown skin. Peel it and cut into thin slices or matchsticks, and use more than you would expect to, for a lot of the heat will cook out. If your green ginger is woody, it will be unpleasant to eat; in such a case, express the juice via a garlic crusher and use that instead. Green ginger is a good addition to fish stocks, to beef stews, to salad dressings, in sauces or gravies with pork or duck. Finely chopped with garlic it is the finest addition of all to finish a multitude of Chinese or oriental stir-fried dishes. It adds a surprise to strawberries, mango and fresh pears . . . once you start using it you'll wonder how you ever managed to cook without it.

Okra: also called ladies' fingers, these green, pointed, curved cones with caps on, can be horrid if the viscous liquid inside isn't dealt with. If it escapes you end up with a slimy mess. You must either cook them gently so it doesn't escape, or get rid of it first, which is the better method. Angling a sharp knife, you cut off the skin of the cap, leaving a sharp peak. When they are all like this, you sprinkle with salt and a little vinegar and leave for an hour or two in a colander, turning from time to time. Then rinse well and cook or deep fry in batter. I prefer them cooked in fresh or tinned tomatoes as they go really well together. With garlic. Of course.

Peppers: also known as capsicums or bell peppers. Thanks to the clever Dutch breeders, there are now four colours red, green, yellow and white. The white one is quite bland in flavour but the others can be somewhat aggressive when eaten raw in salads. A better idea is to slice into strips – not rings – and quickly blanch in boiling water until they are soft but still a bright colour. Drain. This removes the bitterness. They can then be dressed with oil and vinegar, and a salad made like this with several colours of pepper is beautiful to look at. I find it completely unnecessary to take the skin off peppers, something called for often in recipe books and always involving the nonsense of scorching the skins first. Far too much trouble, and often the peppers end up tasting of nothing but charcoal. Far better simply to blanch them as I have outlined. All peppers lend themselves admirably to being stuffed with meat, rice and vegetable mixtures. Sliced peppers stewed in a little olive oil, perhaps with some tomato, make a rugged hot vegetable dish to accompany something that itself lacks a lot of interest, say grilled chicken or plainly cooked lamb chops.

Pumpkin: if you ignore pumpkin you are missing a great treat. The orange colour and earthy sweetness can quite make the appearance of many a meal. Pumpkin can be cooked exactly the same way as potato – boiled, baked, roasted, mashed. All are excellent and all are even better for the accompaniment of lots of butter and some sweet spices, like cinnamon, nutmeg or allspice. It can be very hard to peel, so don't bother – simply cut it into pieces. Squashes are all cooked the same way, no matter what colour or size.

Radiccio: very expensive but this wine-red and white salad ingredient makes a fabulous addition when used for either flavour or colour. You only need a few ounces to make a splash in a salad for 6 people. It has a certain bitterness, so combine it with a sweeter salad plant – some fennel, perhaps, or raw spinach leaves.

Red Cabbage: now becoming more common, red cabbage can be sliced very thinly to make a type of coleslaw but I think it is better served hot. Always fry it in butter or oil first, until brown here and there, and always add a touch of vinegar which helps the colour. You need very little liquid but a fair amount of fat. Best bet is to fry as above, then to add a couple of sliced cooking apples, a spoon or two of vinegar, lots of fatty bacon and a sprinkle of pickling spices. Cover and cook gently for several hours, stirring from time to time. My additions include the usual garlic, some mustard, orange juice and thinly sliced orange peel, juniper berries, bay leaves, gin or a small amount of molasses – but not all together!

Rettish: this long white root vegetable looking like an anaemic carrot is actually a radish; it tastes exactly like the small red-skinned ones and is used the same way. It can be cooked but that doesn't really work in my view.

Spinach: a relatively new addition to the market is a small-leaved variety of spinach which is specially good to eat raw in salads. It is surprisingly sweet with none of the iron-taste of cooked spinach. Very good in combination with crisp bacon cubes or croûtons, and when used to contrast with radiccio, lettuce, fennel – almost anything.

Sweetcorn: the longer you cook it the tougher it gets. And it will also be tough if you put salt in the cooking water. Some say it is good to cook it with some of the outer leaves in the water. You can also slice off the raw kernels and cook those in butter or in a little milk to make creamed corn. A chilli pepper or two goes well with corn and so does, well, you guessed it . . . garlic.

Sweet potatoes: just what they say. Beware of discolouration when peeling by plunging immediately into acidulated water. Better to bake them in their skins or to roast them. Make a purée of the baked potatoes and add cream, rum and cinnamon or nutmeg. Yams are to be treated the same way, but are often nicer because they have either a yellow or pink colour and a waxier texture.

Tomatoes: in case you have not read the introduction, I will repeat that in my opinion there have been no tomatoes available in this country until the last few years. The traditional 'English tomatoes', round and hard and advertised as such, neither look nor taste of tomato. Proper tomatoes are red, lumpy and meaty and large. The marmonde and beefsteak tomatoes now on the market are real tomatoes and I hope that soon no one will eat the orange cotton wool they once thought were tomatoes.

STARTERS

Prawns with Pernod & Kiwi Fruit

Serves 4–6		
Kiwi fruit	6	6
Pernod	2/3 dsp	2/3 dsp
Mayonnaise	4 dsp	4 dsp
Fresh lime	1–2	1–2
Prawns, medium to large	8 oz	225 g
Spinach/radicchio as preferred		

Peel the kiwi fruit thinly and cut into 6 segments, lengthwise. Sprinkle with the Pernod – about ½ a miniature bottle – and leave to chill for at least 30 minutes. Put the mayonnaise into a bowl and finely grate the peel of the lime directly into it, ensuring that you also scrape out and incorporate the zest left inside the grater. Squeeze the juice and add that to the mayonnaise, also, without making it too runny. Chill.

The cooked prawns should be drained if you are using frozen ones; you get more succulent results by defrosting overnight in the refrigerator. Then taste the kiwi fruit; the Pernod flavour should be easily discernable but not overpowering. If you want to add more, do it only teaspoon by teaspoon.

To assemble the dish, put layers of small raw spinach leaves and radicchio at the bottom of a seafood cocktail glass, add the kiwi fruit, then the prawns and top with lime mayonnaise. This also looks terrific when presented more formally in layers on a large white or green plate; arrange the kiwi segments to look like sun rays, pile the prawns in the middle and top with the mayonnaise. Either way, a few extra scrapings of lime peel overall adds a colourful final touch.

Serve cool but not too cold.

Cappelletti with Tuna & Green Peppercorns

Serves 4–6

Pasta dough	1 recipe	1 recipe
Tuna fish, tinned	14–16 oz	400–450 g
Green peppercorns	4 tsp	4 tsp
Green peppercorn brine	4 tsp	4 tsp
Butter	6 oz	175 g

A full recipe of pasta dough (page 68) will make about 6 dozen cappelletti, if each begins as a 2″ (5cm) square of thinly rolled dough. If you must make them much in advance of cooking, or get bored easily, make fewer, of a thicker dough.

To begin, roll out the dough and cut into squares then cover with a barely damp cloth. Mash the tuna roughly with a teaspoon or so of its liquid. White tuna or bonito are the better choices, but the coarser-flavoured tunas work quite as well. Separately, mash 2 teaspoons of the green peppercorns★ together with 2 teaspoons of the brine from their can; mix this with the tuna then divide into even, small piles upon the pasta squares. Don't worry if you have some fish left over – it goes into the sauce. Shape as explained on page 70. This will be a rather moist mixture and thus may split the dough when you twist it. In that case adjust your technique so you leave the stuffed portion of the rolled pasta fairly flat and twist only the arms.

★ Don't use green peppercorns which come in vinegar – for anything! Keep your brined peppercorns in the refrigerator changing the brine when it oxidises and goes black. Or, evict the brine from the start and store the peppercorns in vodka, which itself becomes a useful flavouring ingredient – for Bloody Mary Sauce for instance.

Cook the cappelletti in lots of salted boiling water until they float to the surface. Meanwhile melt the butter and add the remaining two teaspoons of green peppercorns and two teaspoons of their brine. Tip in the left-over tuna fish mixture and heat through until the fish has mushed somewhat. Drain the cappelletti well, divide on plates and pour the sauce around them.

Dill-Pickled Salmon with Mustard Eggs

6 generous servings, twice		
Salmon, fresh	4 lb★	2 kg★
White sugar	3 oz	90 g
Salt	3 oz	90 g
White peppercorns	20	20
Dill fronds	3/4 bunches	3/4 bunches

Bone the salmon, or ask your fishmonger to do so, making two beautiful, even pieces of salmon, skin attached. The salmon should be scaled and well cleaned and wiped dry but not washed unless absolutely filthy and it is very well dried *immediately*.

Rub the back of a knife along the thickest part of the flesh from the head to the tail end of each piece. This will raise the ends of the remaining small bones which may be pulled out using a tweezer or pliers with serrated and pointed ends. The more care taken now, the easier

★ A 2 lb (1 kg) tail piece of salmon or sea trout will make plenty for 6 people and you can use the same amount of pickle as above rather than halving it; cut the amount of dill in half, of course. You might also use dried dill, usually sold as dill tips or dill weed. You would need about 2 oz (50 g) for the full recipe. An expensive recipe? Yes, but *less than half the price of smoked salmon*. It will last in the refrigerator for at least a week but I bet you won't let it do so . . .

the serving, and the more the ensuing enjoyment.

Mix together the salt and sugar, stirring them very well to ensure absolutely even distribution. Crush the peppercorns coarsely and add. Choose a deep dish in which the salmon can lie flat and strew one-quarter of the pickle mixture evenly in it and then add one-quarter of the dill. Put a piece of salmon down next, skin side on the pickle, and strew that with another quarter of pickle and dill. Do that also to the flesh side of the second piece of salmon and lay it on top of its partner flesh to flesh, but head to tail. Cover with the remaining pickle and plenty of dill.

Put plate or a dish that covers the fish on top, and weigh this with at least 6 lbs (3 kg). Leave in a refrigerator for 48 hours; in a cold larder it will be ready in only 24 hours. Turn the fish upside down every 6 hours, more or less. The salt will draw out the liquid in the flesh which in turn dissolves the salt and sugar and preserves the flesh without making it go opaque in the way a marinade, which is acidic, would do.

To serve your dill-pickled salmon – it is a great Scandinavian speciality, known in Sweden as Gravad lax – remove one side from the pickle and scrape away the dill and peppercorns. Take a very sharp, long knife and slice towards the tail, angling the knife downwards so that each slice ends by taking a little flesh from the skin, thus avoiding waste by leaving you with a layer of salmon upon the skin, which only the finest knife-man could remove. Provided your pickle is sweet rather than salty, you might sprinkle each serving with the merest whisper of that, to intensify the dill flavour. In Sweden pickled salmon is served with a sweet mustard sauce which I find perfectly horrid. I have served a mayonnaise spiked with green ginger and accompanied by halved, hard-boiled quails' eggs, and that was much better; but the following idea is simpler, cheaper, and probably as good as you could ever get.

For each serving, scramble a small egg with plenty of butter and perhaps use cream rather than milk. Add a very generous teaspoonful of seed mustard for each egg – don't forget the mustard's heat will quickly cook away. Fold rather than stir the eggs over a medium heat, making long, velvety curds, and remove from the heat whilst still very soft. Chill well before serving.

Mustard scrambled eggs are so good they can be served for breakfast with bacon, put into sandwiches or enjoyed on cold toast as an elegant buffet snack.

Mousselines of White Fish, with Orange Sabayon

Serves 6–9

White fish, raw, trimmed	14 oz	400 g
Nutmeg, ground	pinch	pinch
Onion, chopped	level tsp	level tsp
Garlic, chopped	½ tsp	½ tsp
Lemon juice	2 tsp	2 tsp
Egg whites	2	2
Egg, whole	1	1
Double cream, chilled	¾ pint	425 ml
White pepper/salt	to taste	
Herbs	optional	

For a light end result, reduce the fish, nutmeg, onion, garlic, and lemon juice to an homogeneous paste. It takes seconds in a food processor but can be done with a mortar and pestle. Then add the egg whites and the whole egg, blend well and chill for at least 45 minutes.

The double cream, which must be very cold, is then whipped into the mixture. It is best to do this by hand, to incorporate as much air as possible. A little salt and white pepper may be added at this stage.

Prepare your moulds or timbales by buttering them generously. If you use those of about 3 fl. oz (75 ml) capacity you will be able to make 8 or 9, which gives you extra in case of accidents whilst serving. You can use bigger ones to make just 6. Sprinkle the bottoms with fresh herbs – a frond of fennel or dill, or a little tarragon would be better choices. Stand the moulds in a baking tray then divide the mixture evenly between them. Pour boiling water into the tray until well up the side of the moulds – but do not add so much that the moulds tend to float. Cover with a dome of aluminium foil, sealed tightly around the rim of the tray and put into a preheated oven gas mark 3/325°F/170°C and steam for 25 minutes. Test for doneness by inserting a fine-bladed knife; it will come out clean if all is ready.

Take the mousselines from the oven, carefully take each from the water and let them stand uncovered for at least 5 minutes during which time any free moisture will be re-absorbed. Have ready some warm plates and turn one mousseline on to each. Run a very sharp knife around the edge of the mousseline, right to the bottom of the mould, before inverting.

Now pour a sauce around each one, decorate that with a little more of the herb you put at the bottom of each mould and serve immediately. Take your time for these confections should be warm rather than hot for maximum enjoyment. The voluptuous sabayon can be made while the equally sensual mousselines are cooking and will stand off the heat and stay warm quite long enough for you still to take your time to serve everything beautifully; and it uses the left-over yolks.

Orange Sabayon Sauce

Serves 6		
Orange juice	4 tbsp	4 tbsp
Lemon juice	1 tbsp	1 tbsp
Double cream	8 tbsp	8 tbsp
Egg yolks	2	2
Whole egg	1	1

In a wide bowl – copper is really the best – whisk together all the ingredients until rather frothy then put over boiling water and keep beating until the sauce starts to thicken. Provided you occasionally stir, you can start it heating through without beating to get a quicker start; once the sauce is evenly warm beat until it thickens. Remove from the heat and stir from time to time as it will continue to thicken a little. It should be light and smooth, a mass of tiny bubbles trapped in whipped, orange-cream custard – combined with the mousselines it is the sexiest starter I know.

Pink Fish Pâté

Serves 6		
Peeled prawns	8 oz	225 g
Butter, melted	4 oz	125 g
Lemon juice	to taste	
Double cream	¼ pint	150 ml
Dry white vermouth	capful	capful

If the prawns were bought frozen they should have been defrosted in the refrigerator, as this lets them absorb some of the liquid that is otherwise thrown away. Beware you never buy prawns in a salt-water glaze, as they are always too salty and in this recipe it would be a disaster. Never help prawns defrost by placing in cold or, horror of horrors, in hot water.

Make a purée of the prawns, either by pounding them or whizzing them up in a liquidiser or food processor, adding the melted butter, which should not be too hot. Add the lemon juice also at this stage. Turn into a mixing bowl and allow to cool to tepid or to room temperature but do not let it get it cold enough for the butter to start setting. Whip the cream and fold that into the prawns with the lightest possible hand and finish with the white vermouth. Divide into individual ramekins or put it all onto a prettily contrasted dish. Some melted butter will seal the top, if that is what you want. A sprinkle of fresh dill will add colour and exactly the right extra flavour – in fact a few teaspoonsful of fresh or dried dill tips is a good way to vary this recipe.

Serve with warm, buttered toast or smear onto puff pastry squares; on special occasions top with smoked salmon or some whole prawns and accompany with arcs of poached, seeded cucumber. If you cook these until they are just turning a pale green, then cool them quickly under running cold water they turn the most extraordinarily, beautiful translucent green – I call them jade cucumbers. For variety or economy you can replace half the cream with a soft cream cheese.

Vegetable Patch Pâté with Bloody Mary Sauce

Serves 16–20

Parsnips	2 lb	1 kg
Milk or single cream	¾ pint	425 ml
Butter	2 oz	50 g
Curd or cream cheese	8 oz	250 g
Lemon juice	4 tbsp	4 tbsp
Eggs	8	8
Vegetables, cut into strips	2 lb	1 kg
Vine leaves	as required	

This recipe will make one large party pâté, but you can halve the quantities to make something more suited to a large dinner party. It keeps very well in the refrigerator, anyway.

Scrub the parsnips well and cut them into pieces without peeling them. Poach until tender in the milk (or single cream) and butter. Liquidise the lot, strain, then cool before beating in the cream or curd cheese, eggs and the lemon juice. If you do this when the parsnip purée is hot you lose the advantage of the cheese's texture, and the other vegetables which should make a patchwork of colour in the finished pâté, will simply sink to the bottom.

The variety of additional vegetables should be chosen for colour, texture and flavour – three or four types is enough. Green beans are essential (I use frozen haricots); strips of carrot are excellent. I've also used artichoke bottoms from a tin, green and red peppers (fresh or tinned), stoned black olives (not green ones), turnip, fennel and celeriac. Apart from beans, root vegetables seem to give the best results. None needs to be precooked, but they must be in attractive, long, squared strips or cubes, and each must be independently seasoned. Thus beans, celeriac and fennel should be drenched in garlic, strips of turnip smeared with mustard, artichokes bathed in tarragon vinegar, carrots smothered in finely chopped parsley or rather less thyme or rosemary.

To assemble your Vegetable Patch Pâté, first liberally oil a 3-pint (1½ litre) loaf tin, then line with overlapping vine leaves, their shiny sides outermost, and overhanging the edges.

Pour in a shallow layer of parsnip then arrange your heaviest vegetable in lines lengthwise along the tin. Add more purée, then the next vegetable and so on until the baking tin is filled. Top with vine leaves, interwoven with those from the sides. Stand in boiling water in a roasting tray and cover the pâté with a dome of foil tightly sealed around the baking tin's edge. Bake 1 hour 10 minutes in a preheated oven at gas mark 4/350°F/ 180°C. Let stand 15 minutes, then invert onto a large platter, simply to check that the pâté *will* emerge. If not you will have to do a little scalpel work – but this is most unlikely because of the vine-leaf lining. Line the pâté tin with cling foil or aluminium foil then put back on the pâté, so it stays in shape as it cools. When cool put in the refrigerator to chill thoroughly.

Vegetable Patch Pâté is better served the day after it is made. It should be accompanied by a nice contrasting sauce, and I must say that none is better than my Bloody Mary Sauce.

Bloody Mary Sauce
6 concentrated servings

Reduce a tin of plum tomatoes (14–16 oz/400–450 g) until just a few tablespoons of fairly dry pulp at the bottom of the saucepan – use great care and a low heat. Sieve this to remove the pips. Mix in 1 tablespoon vodka, a *few* sprinkles of celery salt, 1 teaspoon of Worcestershire sauce and a couple of teaspoons of fresh lemon juice. Like the drink, Bloody Mary Sauce should be served ice-cold.

★ ★ ★

In summer this pâté may be made with carrots rather than parsnips, and you can add some thyme whilst they are being poached. If you have fresh herbs in the garden, you might make a layer of these through the middle of your pâté, perhaps with some chopped garlic and a scatter of grated orange peel. If you fancy adding some cubes of ham, chicken or tongue, do so. But then you must call this Farmyard Pâté, which may not be so appealing to your guests!

Pumpkin Gnocchi with Basil Butter

4–6 servings

Pumpkin purée	8 oz	225 g
Nutmeg, ground	½ tsp	½ tsp
Flour, strong white	10 oz	275 g

If you have to make the pumpkin purée, simply boil pumpkin pieces until cooked, scrape the flesh off the skin, then return the vegetable to the heat gently to rid it of excess moisture. If the pumpkin is left wet, you will have to use too much flour to make the pasta-consistency dough and this will hide the sweet, elusive pumpkin flavour.

If you can buy pumpkin purée, you will need only half the usual tin, which contains 16 oz (450 g). But ensure it has not been sweetened for use in pumpkin pie.

Sprinkle the purée with nutmeg then start mixing in the flour until you have a dough that is smooth and does not stick to your hands. The amounts given above are a guide and will depend on the moisture content of the pumpkin as well as that of the flour. Once you have a nice consistency, knead it for a few minutes, then divide it into even pieces – 36 walnut-size, or 72 half that size. Roll each into a ball with floured palms.

Select a big dinner fork, and dip the back of the tines into flour. Take a ball of gnocchi and flatten it on the back of the fork, so that some of the dough is squeezed between the tines. Roll the gnocchi off the fork, from one side to another, to curl it and to accentuate the ridges made by the fork. Instead of rolling the gnocchi off, you can take them between the thumb and forefinger and lift them off, which will also fold them. But do not actually fold your gnocchi in half, as the pocket is needed to hold sauce.

Gnocchi may safely be left, covered, for some hours before cooking them in a great volume of boiling salted water until they rise to the surface. Serve with melted butter flavoured with a crushed clove of garlic and some fresh or dried basil, or with some pesto sauce, which comes from Italy and is often available in tins in delicatessens.

Ravioli with Broad Bean Stuffing

4–6 servings

Pasta dough	1 recipe	1 recipe
Broad beans, blanched	6 oz	175 g
Parmesan cheese	3 oz	85 g
Garlic, crushed	1 clove	1 clove
Lemon juice	1 dsp	1 dsp

If you are using freshly-shelled broad beans, plunge them into boiling salted water for a few minutes, until the skin of each bean starts to soften. Drain. Frozen broad beans need only be defrosted. In both cases, go for smaller, sweeter beans if you have a choice.

In a food processor, place the beans, coarsely grated or chopped cheese, garlic and lemon juice and process until even but still rather coarse. This might also be done by mincing the beans, crushing them in a mortar, or by chopping. The end result should be a paste with chunks, if that makes sense.

Now, if you are a good hand with pastry, one recipe of pasta dough, (page 68) will make 4 trays of ravioli, a total of 144. In other words you should be able to roll 8 sheets of about 14" × 7" (36 cm × 18 cm) from the pasta dough. Of course it is just as acceptable – and faster – to make your ravioli fewer but bigger. If you have a pasta-rolling machine I recommend you to stop at the second to last roller adjustment, as finer pasta tends to split around most fillings. In other words – it's up to you now! Go ahead, make your ravioli as many and as thick or thin as you can bear; frankly, a dozen small ones with a decent sauce is perfectly adequate as a starter per person if there is something substantial to follow, so you can get away with making half quantities of the above recipe.

Leave the ravioli an hour or two to dry, then divide them. If they are a little delicate, keep them in strips. Cook in masses of boiling salted water until they rise to the top. Drain then serve with the following sauce.

Basil-Tomato Sauce

4–6 servings

Plum tomatoes, tinned	28 oz	800 g
Basil, fresh	20 leaves	20 leaves

The tomatoes and their juice should be put into a saucepan and lightly crushed with a fork. Reduce over medium heat until a really thick mush – this will take something like 45–60 minutes and you must beware of burning toward the end. During the short time the ravioli is then cooking, roughly chop the basil leaves and add to the sauce. I don't think this needs salt and pepper and all that, but I suppose some will disagree, even though the parmesan cheese of the stuffing is actually an adequate seasoning for both pasta and sauce.

Divide the sauce between warm plates and serve the raviolis on this brilliant cushion of red and green. The broad bean mixture will just be showing its pretty pale greenness through the pearliness of the pasta, and the combined effect will move even the most bored of eaters.

Some may wish for more sauce but this smaller amount is authentic and you must resist calls for more, or the delicate stuffing will be swamped by tomato.

★ ★ ★

If you only used half a pasta mix or simply couldn't be fagged making 144 ravioli, then also halve the above recipe, using 1 tin of plum tomatoes. If there is no fresh basil about, which is likely, then use about a teaspoon of dried basil per tin of tomatoes, but be careful as dried basil varies enormously and some has a very distinct pepperiness which quickly overwhelms all else.

MAIN COURSES & ACCOMPANIMENTS

Steamed Parsnip Ring

Serves 4–6		
Parsnips	1 lb	450 g
Single cream	½ pint	225 ml
Eggs	4	4
Lemon/lime juice	4 dsp	4 dsp
Salt	to taste	
Dried basil	1–2 tsp	1–2 tsp

First generously butter a decorative ring mould of about 2 pint/1.25 litre capacity, then sprinkle with dried basil, particularly on the base. Scrub the parsnips but do not peel them, and cut into slices. Cook them until tender in the single cream.★ Put both vegetable and cooking liquid into a liquidiser or processor. Add the eggs and citrus juice and process until smooth. Add salt to your personal taste. Ladle the parsnip purée into the mould – it is better if you can wait for it to cool.

Stand the mould in a few inches of boiling water in a pan, cover the mould with a dome of aluminium foil and bake for 20–30 minutes in a preheated oven at gas mark 4/350°F/180°C; the time will depend on how wet your purée was, and the shape and depth of your mould. Don't be tempted to turn up the heat as this might cause the purée to rise too much and all you wish to do is to set the mixture like a custard.

★ If you make this with milk rather than cream you will not get such a good result unless you add a few decent spoonsful of butter. Parsnips are nothing unless they are accompanied by lots of dairy fat.

While it is cooking you might melt some butter and flavour it with garlic juice, which would make a super sauce. Otherwise, once the parsnip mould has been turned out onto a large plate surround it with a rich tomato sauce made by reducing the contents of a 14–16 oz (400–450 g) can of plum tomatoes in their own juice. Once liquidised and sieved this makes a stunning colour and flavour contrast which, in my opinion, does not even need the addition of salt.

Celeriac & Mint Flan

Serves 6–8		
Shortcrust case, pre-baked (approx 10″/25 cm diam.)	1	1
Celeriac, trimmed weight	1 lb	450 g
Milk	¾ pint	425 ml
Garlic clove	1	1
Curd/cream cheese	6 oz	175 g
Lemon/lime juice	4 dsp	4 dsp
Eggs	4	4
Fresh mint leaves	as required	
Nutmeg/allspice	½ tsp	½ tsp

Cube the celeriac quickly, keeping it in lemon juice or salted water to prevent it turning brown. Then cook until tender in the milk. Pour the celeriac and milk into a liquidiser or food processor, add the peeled garlic, the curd or cream cheese, the citrus juice and the eggs, then process until smooth.

Line the pre-baked pastry case with fresh mint leaves or sprinkle with a couple of level teaspoons of dried mint. Gently ladle in the celeriac purée and dust the top with ground nutmeg or allspice, whichever is to hand. Bake for 30 minutes in a preheated oven at gas mark 4/350°F/180°C or until set, but do not brown the top. Eat when lukewarm or cold.

Carrot & Root Ginger Flan

Follow the above method using 1 lb (450 g) scrubbed but unpeeled carrots plus 1″ (2.5 cm) peeled, sliced green ginger cooked together in just ½ pint (275 ml) milk or cream. Purée with cheese, citrus juice and eggs but do not line the case with mint or sprinkle with spice.

★ ★ ★

These vegetable flans were invented to replace the omni-soggy cheese-and-bacon-and-onion-and-everything monstrosities incorrectly called quiches. Both are exceptionally tasty; the carrot and ginger flan has the added attraction of its shiny golden glow. Either would be the perfect centre piece for lunches or buffets.

Noodles with Aubergine Sauce

Serves 4–6

Fresh noodles (page 69)	2 recipes	2 recipes
Salt	1 tsp	1 tsp
Aubergines	2 lb	1 kg
Lemon juice	3 tbsp	3 tbsp
Olive oil	8 tbsp	8 tbsp
Flour	2 dsp	2 dsp
Milk	½ pint	275 ml
Garlic cloves, unpeeled	4–6	4–6
Lemon juice (for sauce)	4 tbsp	4 tbsp
Tomatoes, peeled	1 lb	450 g
Sage, dried	1 tsp	1 tsp
Lemon peel, grated	1 tsp	1 tsp
Parsley, chopped	1 handful	1 handful

Cut the unpeeled aubergines roughly, sprinkle with salt and lemon juice, and leave to drain for a couple of hours. Rinse with cold water then stew gently in a covered pan with oil; as the aubergines start to soften, squash them with a potato masher. Once they are tender, sprinkle the aubergines with the flour, stir, then cook five minutes before adding the milk. Stir continuously until well thickened. Now add the whole unpeeled garlic cloves, lemon juice, peeled tomatoes in thick slices and the dried sage, which should be crumbled finely.

Cover the sauce and simmer it gently for 45 minutes, turning it over from time to time. Once it is creamy and amalgamated, cook the pasta and when that has been put upon hot plates, stir the lemon peel and parsley into the sauce and serve immediately. A small amount of parmesan cheese would not go amiss if sprinkled overall.

This dish starts off looking grey and horrid but finishes up a bewitching pale, smoky pink punctuated with purple aubergine skin, pieces of tomato and the chopped parsley. Do add the garlic in an unpeeled state, just for the pleasure of eating a whole unctuous clove when you find one; and don't be afraid of the robust sage flavour – here it is subtle and invaluable.

Barley Pilaff

Serves 4–6

Pearl barley	8 oz	225 g
Fatty bacon	6 oz	175 g
Celery, cooked	12 oz	350 g
Water or stock	1 pint	550 ml
Plum tomatoes in juice	14–16 oz	400–450 g
Garlic clove	1	1
Celery salt	to taste	

Slice the bacon, which is all the better for being smoked, into strips or into cubes and put into a saucepan or pan. Let it cook until the fat is running very freely, but try not to let it crispen too much. Add the barley and stir constantly until the barley is nicely browned. Slice the cooked celery into strips and add that together with the water or stock. The amount of celery specified is usually that found in a tin of celery, and as this is one vegetable that comes out of a tin in a recognisable state I see nothing wrong with using it; in which case, also use the liquid from the tin as part of the cooking liquid or stock. Stir to mix evenly then cover and leave to cook until all the liquid has disappeared and the barley is tender. This takes about 25 minutes, and if you still have liquid free when the barley is cooked, simply remove the lid and it will soon disappear.

Once the barley is cooked, stir in the tin of tomatoes, and the crushed and chopped clove of garlic. Let heat through then finally season with celery salt. Be very careful for it only needs very little.

This can be served with a salad as a meal in itself for four people. Or it can be spread further as a special vegetable or pilaff with meat, especially poultry.

Barley pilaff cooked with the bacon and a little onion is a tremendously interesting substitute for rice, especially with dishes of game or fatty casseroles and stews.

Stately-Home Baked Beans

Serves 6–8

Haricot or cannelini beans, dried	1 lb	450 g
Plum tomatoes in their juice	28–32 oz	800–1 kg
Onion, sliced	1 or 2	1 or 2
Whole garlic cloves	4–6	4–6
Bay leaves, dry	3	3
Smoked bacon, cubed	8–12 oz	250–375 g
Garlic sausage, sliced	8–12 oz	250–375 g
Red wine (optional)	¼ pint	150 ml

Soak the beans overnight, drain, then cook them in plenty of unsalted water until tender but not falling to pieces. Drain, then put into a casserole that has a good tight fitting lid together with the rest of the ingredients. Although these are called baked beans I always find it better to cook them on top of the stove as this is easier and safer when checking their condition.

Plan to cook at a very low temperature for at least 2 hours, by which time a lot of the fat will have melted and been absorbed, and some of the beans will have dissolved to form, with the tomatoes, a rich thick sauce. If the mixture is a little dry, then you can always add more tomato or some water. If you leave baked beans to be reheated the next day the flavour is even more spectacular. For a final extraordinary touch, stir in some red wine. This was Clare Latimer's hint, who is Food Editor of *Woman's World*; I laughed when she suggested it was good in tinned baked beans, too. In fact it is amazingly good, but none of us can work out why.

This is called Stately-Home Baked Beans because I demonstrated how to make it on a barbecue at Hagley Hall, the stunning stately home of Lord and Lady Cobham, when it opened for the summer season. Lady Cobham snatched the leftovers to serve in the 'Big House' so I reckoned it deserving of the name.

Trout with Celeriac & Hazelnut Stuffing

Per person		
Trout	8–12 oz	250–350 g
Celeriac, peeled	4 oz	125 g
Hazelnuts, toasted	1 oz	25 g
Lemon juice	few tsp	few tsp
Garlic	small clove	small clove
White wine or vermouth	2/3 tsp	2/3 tsp
Butter	2 tsp	2 tsp
Soured cream	optional	

The trout do not need to be boned but if you would prefer this, instructions are given on page 77. Ensure the hazelnuts are really well toasted right through then chop them roughly, rubbing off the skin first if you are fussy. Grate the peeled celeriac directly into a little pool of lemon juice and turn it as you go to ensure it is well coated, or it will discolour. Squeeze the garlic's juice directly into the celeriac, then mix in the chopped hazelnuts using two forks to pull rather than to stir. Extend the fish cavity right to the tail and fill with the stuffing★.

Lay the trout on buttered foil and sprinkle with a little white wine or vermouth and a pat of butter. Seal and bake at gas mark 4/350°F/180°C for 15 minutes. Serve.

For the nicest presentation quickly remove the skin of the uppermost side of the trout, using a broad bread and butter knife. Then dot on some blobs of soured cream.

★ To make each trout look more professionally prepared you should cut off all the fins before it is stuffed. If you prefer poached trout, make a little stock with the offcuts and the bones of the trout and use that; it is very spectacular if you wrap such fish in vine leaves. With or without, poach in just a little water, covered, in the oven for the same time as above. Of course, it will take longer if the fish is still chilled, so adjust accordingly.

Princess of Wales Salmon

Serves 4–6

Salmon tail piece	2 lb	1 kg
Leeks, trimmed weight	1 lb	450 kg
Butter	3 oz	90 g
Seed mustard	1–2 oz	30–60 g
Parsley	1 bunch	1 bunch
White vermouth or wine	2 dsp	2 dsp

Carefully open and bone the piece of salmon. If you are busy, or timid, ask your fishmonger to take the two sides off the bone for you – but take the bones home.

Ideally, remove any smaller bones that remain in the flesh, too – see the Dill-Pickled Salmon recipe (page 21). Skin the salmon by putting skin side down in shallow boiling water for 40 seconds; this should be enough to allow you to peel off the skin. This step is not absolutely necessary, but I think the fish looks nicer, and so does the plate when you have finished eating. Spread the insides of the salmon with seed mustard, preferably one made with wine, then leave in a cool place.

Make ½ pint (275 ml) or so of fish stock by simmering the salmon skin and bones in water, or water and wine, for 20 minutes. Drain and reserve. Slice the trimmed leeks very thinly, rinse thoroughly, then cook until just softening in the fish stock. Drain, again reserving the liquid. Make a thick purée of the warm leek with the butter. If you need extra moisture, add a little of the salmon/leek stock. Spread half the purée on the two pieces of salmon and sandwich them together – leek to leek as 'twere. Make a bed of parsley on a large piece of foil, sprinkle this with dry white vermouth or white wine and put the salmon on this. Sprinkle with a little more alcohol then close the foil tightly, leaving plenty of space above the fish so the steam made by the wine and parsley can circulate. Bake in a preheated oven at gas mark 4/350°F/180°C for 30–40 minutes – the longer time if the salmon came straight from the refrigerator. For special meals you could wrap the salmon in puff pastry and bake it for the same amount of time but at a slightly higher temperature to start with to get the pastry going.

A few minutes before the salmon is ready, reheat the remaining leek purée and thin it with some salmon/leek stock until a nice pouring consistency – but do not boil the purée or sauce, or keep it hot for too long, or you will lose the bright greenness of the leeks.

Serve the Princess of Wales salmon in slices with the sauce at one side. This is particularly good when served cold, but don't serve it direct from the refrigerator as this masks much of the subtle interplay of flavours.

This dish was invented to celebrate the announcement of the Princess of Wales' pregnancy – did you know that fish is good for mothers to be? Although still a special occasion fish to most of us, salmon is really dropping in price and will be under £2 for a pound in the very near future as so much of it is being farmed, and I defy anyone to find any taste difference between wild and farmed salmon. The combination of leeks, butter and mustard goes so well with fish that you might like to try it with a tail piece of cod or other large fish. Or you could stuff a whole, boned haddock or whiting, a much underrated fish nowadays. Isn't it odd that in large Victorian households servants refused to eat salmon more than three times a week, while whiting, which is now usually given only to cats, were then served with their tails in their mouths as a great delicacy at the master's table.

Keemun Chicken

Serves 4–6		
Chicken, cleaned weight	3 lb	1.5 kg
Keemun tea leaves (dry)	1 oz	25 g
Mint, dried	2 heaped tsp	2 heaped tsp
Water, boiling	½ pint	275 ml
Orange juice	2 fl. oz	50 ml
Lemon juice	2 fl. oz	50 ml
Dried apricots	4 oz	125 g
Butter	2 oz	50 g

Cut the chicken into 10 neat pieces and remove the skin from each, except for that on the wings. Put the tea leaves and the dried mint into a bowl and pour on the boiling water; leave to stand 7–9 minutes. Meanwhile arrange the chicken pieces on the bottom of a casserole in which they can all lie flat. Pour on the orange and lemon juice. Strain the mint tea mixture and add the liquid to the dish, and jiggle it somewhat to mix it with the citrus juices. Cover and let marinate for 8 hours, turning the chicken from time to time. Add the dried apricots*, cut in half, for the last two hours.

When you are ready to cook your Keemun chicken, dot the chicken pieces with butter, cover the dish with foil and cook in a preheated oven at gas mark 4/350°F/ 180°C oven for no more than an hour; if you overcook this, the fragile flavour will disappear. Serve on a pilaff of plain rice or toasted barley (see p. 35).

*I know apricots are expensive but I often find people have some left over and don't know what to do with them. This dish is based on a famous Armenian way of cooking pheasant, using green tea with many extra-ordinary other ingredients. If you like the combination of apricots and mint, use them mixed with rice or barley to stuff lamb, chicken, pigeons, ham or vine leaves.

Chicken Supremes
in Lime Coconut Sauce

Serves 4		
Chicken supremes (page 42)	4	4
Lime juice, fresh	3 fl. oz	75 ml
Dry white vermouth	2 fl. oz	50 ml
Green ginger, peeled	1 oz	25 g
Green chilli pepper, small	1	1
Creamed coconut, dry weight	7 oz (approx)	200 g (approx)
Lime peel, freshly grated	1 lime	1 lime

Once the supremes have been prepared, mix together the lime juice and the vermouth. If you don't have dry white vermouth, use a dry white wine rather than another type of vermouth. Slice the peeled green ginger then squeeze the juice from the slices using a garlic crusher. Add the ginger juice to the other liquids.

Arrange the supremes in a baking dish and pour this marinade over them.

Cut the top from the chilli pepper and remove the seeds from inside. Then cut the pepper into very thin slices and sprinkle that over the chicken. Wash your hands very thoroughly or you run the risk of getting the sting of the pepper into your eyes accidentally. Leave the chicken to marinate for several hours, turning from time to time.

Cover the baking dish with foil and put into a gas mark 4/350°F/180°C oven for 30 minutes if the meat was at room temperature, 10 minutes longer if it was chilled. Pour off and reserve the juices and return the chicken to the oven, covered, at the lowest heat. Chop the coconut into a small saucepan, add the strained chicken juices and melt together over a medium heat – do not boil or use high heat or the sauce will curdle. Pour the sauce over the chicken and serve at the table from the baking dish. Sprinkle freshly grated lime peel over each serving. A purée of sweet potato goes well with this, but add colour to the plate with some chinese leaves cooked with garlic or some okra in tomato sauce.

Cutting a Supreme of Chicken

A supreme of chicken is a boneless breast, usually with the first joint of the wing, including its bone, attached.

Buy breasts which have been cut long, that is, which are whole and entire. When the meat is completely defrosted, first remove the skin by pulling from the pointed end towards the wishing bone end. Then cut out the wishing bone. Return to the pointed end and use a knife to ease the flesh away from the rib cage. Angling the blade towards the bones, gently cut away the flesh and be careful not to separate the main muscle from the long thin fillet that lies on its inside. When you get down to the joint of the wing and rib cage, cut through this and you have your boneless supreme. All that remains is for you to trim it nicely of pieces of fat and to take off all but the first joint of the wing.

Open-Plan Chicken Pie
with Flyaway Phyllo Pastry

Serves 6–8 easily

Phyllo pastry (page 72)	1 recipe	1 recipe
Chicken, jointed	3 lb	1.5 kg
Milk	1 pint	550 ml
Small onion, sliced	1	1
Bayleaf	1	1
Sweet herbs	optional	
Butter (for sauce)	2 tbsp	2 tbsp
Flour	2 tbsp	2 tbsp
Extra butter or oil		
Lemon peel, grated	1–2 tsp	1–2 tsp
Spinach, fresh or	1½ lb	750 g
Spinach leaf, frozen	1 lb approx	500 g approx

The beauty of this really spectacular-looking dish is that it can all be prepared in advance. As well, the size of the chicken and amount of spinach are very flexible, so don't waste time weighing every chicken in the market or looking for an extra leaf of spinach; but a bigger chicken gives a more substantial pie.

The sensible way to approach the construction of this is to have the chicken cooking whilst you make the phyllo pastry. So, have the chicken in conveniently sized pieces and put them with the onion into the milk together with a bay leaf and some sweet herbs like marjoram and parsley if you have them. Gently poach the chicken until it will come away from the bone, but stop well before it becomes stringy through overcooking – 45 minutes is probably enough time, unless your bird was more decrepit than you thought. Drain off the well-flavoured milk and reserve. When the flesh is cool enough to handle, flake it off in large pieces. Cover and keep cool.

In the meantime you should have made your phyllo and then rolled and cut 10–12 sheets approx. 12″ × 8″ (30 cm × 20 cm) – always cover them with a slightly dampened cloth if you have to leave them for any time.

On a baking tray layer 5 or 6 phyllo* sheets upon each other, bathing each with melted butter or a mixture of butter and olive oil as you go. Put this into a pre-heated oven at gas mark 4/350°F/180°C for 20 minutes or until the pastry is well risen and browned. If there are any edges that appear in danger of scorching spray or paint with water during the cooking.

Now repeat the process with the other sheets of phyllo, but this time cut a diamond pattern through the top two sheets before baking. If the first lot did not crumple and curl at the edges then turn up the heat of the oven a smidge, and be even more assiduous about watching for burn. Keep both pastry squares out of harm's way. Next you must make the sauce for the chicken.

Melt the butter in the saucepan, add the flour and stir and cook a few minutes without letting it brown. Whisk in the flavoured milk and stir until thickened. Simmer at least 15 minutes, and if you think the sauce too thin, do this without a lid to let it reduce somewhat. Then add lemon peel to get an attractive, balanced flavour. Keep warm with some cling film on its surface.

When you are getting close to serving time, wash and drain the spinach if you are using fresh, pull it into pieces about 2″ (5cm) square and cook quickly (using no water) for a few minutes until it is wilted. Drain well. Cook frozen spinach as directed and drain well.

The work is now done and you can go away and play or talk to your guests. Once you decide they must be fed, put the chicken pieces into the sauce and heat

---

*If you can buy phyllo pastry, then use it by all means, but there is nothing quite like serving your own, even if it is nowhere near as thin as the commercial type.

through. Put the phyllo pastry into the oven and heat through. And when those are ready toss the spinach in some hot butter to heat that.

Put the bottom layer of pastry on a suitable platter and cover with the drained, buttered spinach. Ladle on the chicken in its sauce, then top with the second, more decorative piece of pastry. Take to the table and serve in squares. It cuts far more easily than you expect.

Lamb Chops on Toast

I know this sounds rather bizarre, or worse, ordinary, but I assure you it will quickly become a favourite. It makes a double lamb chop (two undivided chops cut across the back rather than one extra thick chop) into a far more substantial choice for lunch or a light supper.

For each person you take a medium-thick slice of good, wholemeal bread and smear that well with seed mustard – *moutard de meaux, dijon*, or similar. Try to choose one that is mixed with wine, which ingredient will be revealed on the label. Cover the mustard with fresh mint leaves or with a good sprinkle of dried mint. Both mustard and mint lose much of their savour when cooked, so you must be generous.

Then put the double chop on top and curl in its ends, trimming if you have to do so. Put the construction onto a baking tray and place in a preheated medium oven gas mark 4/350°F/180°C. After 10 minutes turn the chop over and cook another 10 minutes.

This will give you pink flesh which is the best way of eating lamb; but cook it on a little if you prefer it more well done.

The juices of the meat will have soaked into the bread, and the edges will have toasted and crisped through a combination of fat from the chops and the oven's heat. It couldn't be simpler or more unexpected, could it?

Pan Kebabs

Serves 2		
Boneless leg of lamb	12 oz	350 g
Cooking oil	1 dsp	1 dsp
Lemon juice	4 dsp	4 dsp
Coriander, ground	1 tsp	1 tsp
Cumin, ground	1 tsp	1 tsp

Cut the lamb meat into cubes, mix the other (marinade) ingredients together, pour over the meat, toss well. Then cover and leave for 3 or 4 hours.★

To cook these kebabs without the trouble of skewers, you must have a non-stick pan. Heat it until really hot, then drain the lamb and fry the cubes for 8–10 minutes stirring all the time. When the kebabs are cooked or pink enough for your taste, quickly sprinkle with whatever marinade was left plus a little extra lemon juice.

Serve pan kebabs on white rice with a tomato, cucumber and green pepper salad. Or pre-heat some pocketed pitta bread, stuff with some lettuce, tomato and pitted black olives, and put the pan kebabs in on top.

Another interesting combination is lamb with orange and rosemary. Make a marinade of 2 parts orange juice, 2 parts white wine and 1 part lemon juice for the kebabs, perhaps adding crushed garlic. Be generous with the marinade – the kebabs can almost swim this time. Thirty minutes before serving pour off the marinade and reduce it over a medium heat until almost syrupy. Sprinkle in some fresh or dried rosemary, let that flavour develop to your taste then strain the spikes out. Cook the kebabs as above and just before serving whisk a few teaspoonsful of butter into the sauce, put that onto the plates and arrange the kebabs nicely on top of the sauce.

★ You cannot make lamb kebabs without marinating the meat for some time, as the leg of lamb invariably toughens when cooked at a high heat unless so treated.

Pocketed Shoulder of Lamb with Red Peppers

Serves 4–6		
Shoulder of lamb	as it comes	
Red peppers, trimmed	8 oz	200 g
Butter	1 oz	25 g
Garlic clove	1	1
Dry white vermouth	2 dsp	2 dsp
Fresh lemon juice	2 dsp	2 dsp
Hot (Hungarian) paprika	1 tsp	1 tsp

De-stalk and core the red peppers and cut them into strips without bothering to be neat and tidy. Throw these into boiling water until they start to soften. Drain and put into a liquidiser or food processor with the butter and the garlic and process into a purée. Add the other ingredients and mix. Whilst that cools pocket the shoulder of lamb, as explained on page 76, by removing the shoulder-blade and extending the resultant cavern down parallel to the remaining bone.

Spoon in the purée then close the aperture with tooth-picks; but do it this way – insert the toothpick into the underside of the bottom flap of meat, then twist it over and down through the top half, angling it back and out through the bottom. If you go in through the top you will never get a good seal unless you sew it up, and who wants to do that. Oh yes, and if you split the skin whilst removing the bone, weave that together with tooth-picks too. Rest the cobbled edge on a large potato or take off the knuckle end of the shoulder and use this as a rest, so the sauce does not dribble out during roasting. If you have some more lemon or lime, squeeze this over the joint then roast it at 20 minutes per lb plus 10 minutes in a preheated oven at gas mark 4/350°F/180°C. Let it rest for 10–15 minutes before you cut it, so the juices stay in the meat when you carve.

Spiced Coffee Butterfly of Lamb

Serves 4–8

Leg of lamb, butterflied (page 76)	(size as it comes)	
Wine or water	½ pint	275 ml
Peel of orange	1	1
Cinnamon stick	1	1
Clove	1	1
Crushed cardamom seeds	2 pods	2 pods
Bay leaves	2	2
Strong instant coffee powder★	1 dsp	1 dsp
Sugar	to taste	

Once you have de-boned your lamb, put the wine or water into a saucepan together with the orange, spices and bay leaves and simmer for 5 minutes. Add the instant coffee powder★ and, if you like, a little sugar, for sometimes the cardamom flavour can be intrusive. Let this cool, then cut a criss-cross pattern through the fat side of the lamb and pour over the strained marinade.

Leave this in a cool place for at least 3 hours; but it is better if you can leave it the whole day. Either way pour the marinade back over the meat or turn the meat from time to time. When ready, pour off most of the marinade and reserve. Put the lamb into a pre-heated oven gas mark 4/350°F/180°C to cook for 15–20 minutes per lb plus an extra 15–20 minutes depending whether you like your lamb very pink, pink or well done. During the cooking, pour on some of the marinade at regular intervals, but watch you don't sog the meat.

Once cooked, remove from the oven and let sit for 15 minutes before cutting. While it is setting, pour off the pan juices, add to the rest of the marinade and reduce until rich

★ Don't be too surprised at the use of instant coffee; it would be silly to use real coffee as it would lose much of its finer, more expensive flavours.

and syrupy. Adjust the flavour by adding a little wine, or some more orange, and just before serving, whisk in a few teaspoonful of butter.

Pebble Mill's Painted Party Pie

Serves 8–10		
Chicken livers	8 oz	225 g
Small onion, chopped	1	1
Garlic clove, large	1	1
Allspice, ground	1 tsp	1 tsp
Nutmeg, ground	½ tsp	½ tsp
Thyme, dried	1 tsp	1 tsp
Rosemary, dried	½ tsp	½ tsp
Juniper berries	6	6
Belly of pork, trimmed	12 oz	350 g
Smoked bacon	8 oz	225 g
Mushrooms, large	8 oz	225 g
Eggs	6–8	6–8
Puff pastry	1 lb	450 g
Black pepper	generous amount	
Egg for glaze	1	1
Brandy	optional	

Put the chicken livers, onion, garlic, spices and herbs into a liquidiser or food processor and reduce to a purée. If you are flush, a dessertspoonful or two of brandy might also be added. Cut the trimmed (that is boneless and skinless) belly of pork into cubes. If the bacon is sliced, cut it into strips, if in a piece cut it also into cubes. Add the belly and the bacon to the purée in a food processor and make an even but coarsely textured mixture. If you don't own a processor, then mince or chop coarsely the two meats before adding them to the chicken liver base.

49

Line a baking dish that is several inches deep (5–6 cm) with two thirds of the pastry and brush this with the white of the egg you will use for glazing. Stand a pie funnel in the centre of the pastry. Put half the meat mixture evenly into the pastry shell then break in the eggs. If they do not join to cover the entire surface, add one or two more. Pepper freely. Sprinkle over the remaining meat. Slice the peeled mushrooms thickly and arrange them on top. Cover with puff pastry, make an extra rim about an inch wide from the offcuts and put it round the edge, on top, slash a few air vents, then paint the pastry (page 74) in a manner suited to the occasion. Glaze. Bake in a preheated oven at gas mark 7/420°F/220°C for 15 minutes then reduce to gas mark 4/350°F/180°C for another hour. Serve cold the following day.

PUDDINGS

Fruit on Toast

Like Lamb Chops on Toast, this recipe was perfected when I was demonstrating at the Ideal Home Exhibition this year. Often we see lovely plums or pears, peaches or nectarines for sale; but they are either a bit green, very expensive, or both. I wanted to find a way to enjoy them without breaking the bank or getting a stomach ache. This is my solution.

For each serving you must start with a nice slice from a white-milk loaf or a Vienna loaf, as these are also made with milk; milk gives all bread a sweeter flavour and more cake-like texture. Other high-quality styles of white bread can also be used, or slices of brioche, but don't use sliced, white sandwich loaf or you will be disappointed. At least, I was.

Now – generously butter each slice, sprinkle with demerara sugar, dust with cinnamon and trim off the crusts. I find that plums and green gages work particularly well, but I have also had success with apricots, peaches and nectarines. Cut the fruit in half, stone or core, and place cut side down on the bread. Make some deep cuts in the fruit and into those insert slithers of butter. Sprinkle with more sugar and cinnamon. Lay them into a baking dish rather than onto a baking tray, as syrup and juices will form and you should reserve this.

Put the dish under a lowish grill or in a medium oven until the fruit has softened and the edge of the bread is crisp and brown – up to 20 minutes depending on the state of the fruit and the heat of the oven. There are no rules and it is almost impossible to go too wrong.

Let the toasts cool somewhat, then serve on nice plates with the syrup that has formed and a little cream. A sprinkle of rum or brandy or some suitable liqueur would harm nothing but your budget.

Jasmine Tea Ice Cream

Serves 6–8 easily		
Milk	½ pint	275 ml
Jasmine tea leaves (dry)	1 oz	25 g
Sugar	5 oz	150 g
Cornflour/arrowroot	1 level dsp	1 level dsp
Egg yolks	2	2
Salt	pinch	pinch
Whipping/double cream	½ pint	275 ml

Boil the milk and pour over the jasmine tea leaves. Stir and let stand 7–9 minutes, turning from time to time. Strain well then make back up to the original volume with cold milk. Mix the sugar, cornflour★ (or arrowroot), egg yolks and salt together in a saucepan and whisk in the tea-milk. Stir over a medium heat until thickened, reduce heat and simmer at least 5 minutes or until all trace of a starchy flavour has fled. Strain this tea custard to ensure there is no lumpiness and leave to cool but not set with clingfilm pressed to its surface.

Once the custard is at room temperature, whip the cream lightly and fold the two together. Freeze. It is not necessary to re-beat this ice cream halfway through the freezing process but you will get a finer textured end result if you do so. If your freezer is slow you will find this half-way beating mandatory. Check about an hour after you have put the ice cream into the freezer, and when it is solid about the edges but mushy in the centre, remove it and give it a thorough but brief beating to even out the texture and temperature. Get it back into the freezer as soon as possible.

Remove the ice cream from the freezer and put it into the refrigerator about 30–45 minutes before serving.

★ The use of cornflour or arrowroot to save an egg custard from curdling is not such a cheat as you may think. It is used in the classic french pastry filling called frangipane.

Earl Grey's Sorbet with Oriental Fruits

Serves 6–8

Earl Grey's tea (dry)	1 oz	25 g
Boiling water	1 pint	550 ml
Sugar	5 oz	150 g
Lime or lemon juice	3/4 tbsp	3/4 tbsp
Egg whites (optional)	1 or 2	1 or 2

Pour the boiling water onto the tea leaves and let stand 7 minutes. Strain well then make the tea back up to the original volume by adding cold water. Dissolve the sugar in this warm liquid, then add lime or lemon juice. Be careful not to overwhelm the perfume of the tea – the exact balance will depend on the Earl Grey's tea you choose.

Pour the liquid into a suitable container and set in the freezer. After an hour it should be set at the edges and mushy in the centre, and at that stage it needs to be mashed and beaten into an even consistency. If you use a food processor you will also add air, which lightens the sorbet. You may re-freeze as it is, but you will find sorbets melt very easily when served. It is better to whip up one or two egg whites and to fold them into the beaten sorbet. Not only will this prevent ice crystals forming, it stops the sorbet forming a puddle on the plate.

Take the sorbet from the freezer and put into the refrigerator at least 30 minutes before serving. A sorbet should always be served soft and mushy rather than icy cold, a condition which masks most of the delicate flavour you have strived to preserve.

Have some regard for the sorbet's aristocratic pedigree when you serve it. Present it with style, as the centre piece of a colourful arrangement of exotic fruits, each marinated separately . . . some lychees sprinkled with rosewater, a couple of peeled and stoned fresh dates soaked in vodka, a slice or two of chilled tangerine, a sliced kumquat, some kiwi fruit doused with cointreau . . .

Ceylon Tea & Pineapple Sorbet

Serves 6

Ceylon tea leaves or bags	1 oz	25 g
Boiling water	½ pint	250 ml
Dried mint	1 tsp	1 tsp
Sugar	4 oz	125 g
Pineapple juice, unsweetened	½ pint	250 ml
Egg whites (optional)	1 or 2	1 or 2

Pour the boiling water onto the tea leaves or tea bags and the mint. Brew 3 minutes if using bags, 5 minutes if using leaves. Drain and strain well and make liquid back to original volume with cold water. Dissolve the sugar in the liquid, add the pineapple juice and check for sweetness, remembering the frozen sorbet will taste far less sweet.

Freeze this until mushy, then proceed as explained in the last recipe. Don't forget to allow the sorbet to soften in the refrigerator before serving. If you find you have taken it out too soon, it is easy to put it back into the freezer to firm it up, but it is damned difficult to soften it quickly and evenly.

The delicious combination of tea and pineapple goes very well with other things tropical. It is perfect scooped onto rings of fresh pineapple, or onto cheeks of mango. It makes a tantalising combination with ice creams, provided they are real, dairy ice creams, made with cream and natural flavourings rather than with palm oil.

To be right in vogue – and I'm sure you would *like* to be right in vogue – you might consider serving a carousel of sorbets and ice cream, beautiful mounds of several types. In fact a serving of this sorbet, plus one of Earl Grey's Sorbet and some Jasmine Tea Ice Cream, set on a purée of fruit (raspberry, mango or blackcurrant) and a dribble of stem ginger syrup over the top would get you absolutely top points.

Broken-Down Japonais

Serves about 16		
Egg whites	6	6
Sugar	12 oz	350 g
Milk	½ pint	275 ml
Egg yolks	6	6
Sugar	4 oz	125 g
Cornflour	1 dsp	1 dsp
Unsalted butter	14 oz	400 g
Praline (page 74)	8 oz	250 g
Instant coffee powder	1 tbsp	1 tbsp
Sugar for caramel	6 oz	175 g

Prepare a meringue mixture by first whisking the egg whites then beating in the sugar until the meringue is glossy and stiff. Line the bottom of two 9″ (22 cm) sandwich tins with buttered greaseproof paper or foil and divide the mixture evenly between the two. Put into an oven at gas mark ½/250°F/120°C and bake for 2 hours, exchanging their positions in the oven every so often. Turn off the oven and leave with the door closed until absolutely cold.

Continue by making a butter cream, known in better circles as creme au beurre a l'Anglais – except this time it is à la Glynn Christian. Mix the milk, egg yolks and sugar together in a saucepan, then use some of this to make a paste with the cornflour. Stir that back then heat gently until thickened and cook another 5 minutes to remove any trace of flouriness. Let this cool, with cling film on its surface. At this stage, whip the butter with an electric beater until it resembles the texture of the custard; slowly beat the butter into the custard, about a dessertspoonful at a time; this shouldn't curdle, because of the cornflour, but I guess it might if you have been mean with the cornflour and precipitate with the butter. In this case, whisk in a few dessertspoonsful of tepid melted butter, which should reverse the reverse.

Once the butter is incorporated, stir in the praline, which is all the better for being coarse rather than fine, then the coffee powder. There is yet another process before you can assemble the monster.

Melt the remaining amount of sugar over gentle heat until a golden brown and quite clear. Pour that onto a lightly oiled baking sheet and gently tip it back and forth so the sugar spreads as thinly as possible before it starts to set. Let that cool, too.

Once the meringues are cool, the butter cream is mixed and the caramel sheet is also cold, you may proceed. Take the crisper of the two meringues (one is always crisper unless you have been able to bake them side by side) and turn it onto a large, beautiful plate. Remove the greaseproof or foil, of course. Break up the other meringue roughly and mix that into the praline/coffee butter cream. Spread that over the intact meringue and smooth it evenly.

Put the point of a sharp knife on the centre point of the sheet of caramel and bash firmly. The sugar should shatter into spikes and flakes. If not, pierce firmly in a number of other places until you have about 16 or so fairly even but irregularly shaped fragments. Plunge them attractively about the edge of the construction. Left over fragments can be crushed and sprinkled into the centre. At last . . . you can serve and eat.

If you have made a very crisp meringue, you may leave the Broken-Down Japonais for a day in a cool place – but don't put it into a refrigerator. But it really is better if put together just a few hours before it is consumed, when the meringue and praline in the topping will still have much of their crunch. It is frightfully rich, as you can imagine, but not half as sweet as you might imagine.

★   ★   ★

I suppose you want an explanation of the name. The real Japonais includes the same components but requires 3 rounds of meringue, a butter cream that is bound to curdle unless you are a four-star genius, and a way with making things round and smooth that is rare. Thus I broke down the recipe into easier techniques and construction methods. And it is also guaranteed to break down any diet known to man, woman or beast.

Praline Pavlova with Kiwi Fruit

Serves about 8		
Egg whites	6	6
Caster sugar	12 oz	350 g
Malt vinegar	1 large tsp	1 large tsp
Vanilla essence	1 large tsp	1 large tsp
Double cream	½ pint	275 ml
Praline (page 74)	6–8 oz	200–250 g
Kiwi fruit	4–6	4–6

Beat the egg whites, which must be at room temperature, until they hold firm peaks. Gradually beat in the sugar and keep beating until the mixture is very thick and glossy; you really cannot expect to achieve the proper result without an electric beater. Fold in the vinegar and vanilla essence.

The mixture can be arranged on a slightly wet baking tray, pushed roughly into a sculpted circle with a spatula. But I think it is better if you line a straight-sided dish of at least 10″ (25 cms) diameter with buttered greaseproof paper or with foil and pour the mixture evenly in to that. You get a more reliable end product, and don't risk syrup running all over the place if you haven't beaten in the sugar properly.

Bake in a preheated oven at gas mark ¼/225°F/110°C for 1½ hours, and leave in the oven until completely cool – perhaps overnight. For a pinky brown finish cook at a slightly higher temperature. Tip the pavlova onto a suitable plate, remove the greaseproof paper or foil then invert again, to place the crisp crust on top. If you have baked on a sheet, simply loosen the pavlova with a spatula and slide it onto a plate. Don't worry about cracks and splits – they are part of pavlovas. Whip the double cream and flavour highly with the praline to your taste then swirl it upon the pavlova with little regard for prettiness. Slice the peeled kiwi fruit thickly and arrange the pieces around the edge. Keep cool but do not refrigerate.

★   ★   ★

Unless a meringue base is like marshmallow in the middle it is *not* a pavlova.

Hello Sailor!
Bread & Butter Pudding

Serves 4–6

White toast, buttered	6–8 slices	6–8 slices
Cinnamon, ground	2–3 tsp	2–3 tsp
Banana, very ripe	1	1
Raisins or sultanas	2 oz	50 g
Lime, grated rind and juice	1	1
Eggs	2	2
Sugar, brown or white	3 tbsp	3 tbsp
Black rum	6 tbsp	6 tbsp
Milk	1 pint	550 ml

Choose almost any white bread other than that from a sliced sandwich loaf, as this will become a nasty mush. The toast should be lavishly buttered and sprinkled with cinnamon. Remove the crusts and slice the toast into fingers. In a small bowl, slice the banana, mix in the raisins or sultanas, grate in the rind of a fresh lime then squeeze its juice and add that. Mix well. Beat the two eggs together, then add the sugar, rum and milk.

Arrange the spicy toast and the fruit in layers in an oblong or square baking dish, remembering that the bread will swell. Pour in the custard mixture and let this sit for 20–30 minutes, gently pushing the top layer under the liquid from time to time until all is absorbed. Then pour over any remaining lime juice from the banana/raisin mixture. Bake at gas mark 4/350°F/180°C for 50 minutes, or until the custard is set and the toast is crisp and golden on top. Serve warm rather than hot, with lashings of cream flavoured with more black rum.

* * *

I first called this Prince of Wales Pudding, for the idea of including banana came from His Royal Highness. The combination of bananas, rum and lime in a bread and butter pudding so astonished novelist Angela Huth she almost drove off a motorway when it was broadcast. The new name is chosen simply for sensation, which is exactly what you will find this to be – but do not mention it to Miss Huth if she is driving.

Mexican Bread & Butter Pudding

Serves 4–6		
White bread, stale	10 slices	10 slices
Melted butter	4 oz	125 g
Barbados sugar	12 oz	350 g
Cinnamon, ground	2 tsp	2 tsp
Water	½ pint	275 ml
Butter	3 oz	90 g
Cottage cheese	4 oz	125 g
Pinenuts/hazelnuts, chopped	3 oz	90 g

The bread should be from a medium-sized loaf, but not from a sliced sandwich loaf as this will go mushy. Cut away the crusts then paint the slices with the melted butter, ensuring each is well and truly saturated. Place on a baking tray and bake in a preheated oven until brown and sizzling at gas mark 6/400°F/200°C.

In the meantime, mix together the sugar, cinnamon and water and boil together for 4 minutes to make a nice syrup; if you cannot get real barbados sugar, use the lighter demerara. Failing that use one of the coloured soft sugars. If there is some melted butter left over, use that to brush the inside of a 3 pint (2 litre) ovenproof dish, otherwise use a very little of the second quantity of butter.

When the baked toast is cool enough to handle, place all the ingredients into the dish in layers, starting with toast and adding crumbled cheese, flakes of butter, chopped nuts and the syrup. Try to finish the top with some of the nuts. If there is still some melted butter left pour that over the top, too. Bake at gas mark 4/350°F/180°C for 20 minutes or until it is well heated through, the toasts are swollen and the nuts are lightly browned.

Serve with a hot fruit sauce. Apple sauce would be very good. Or make an old fashioned jam sauce by melting a good fruit jam with a little water. Apricot or peach would work nicely. Needless to say, although not easily found in a Mexican village, lashings of cream would not go astray if you had some. As pinenuts are scarce and expensive, hazelnuts do very well instead.

Coconut Pasta with Orange-Almond Syrup

4–6 servings		
Pasta dough	½ mixture	½ mixture
Coconut, dessicated	3 oz	90 g
Sugar	2 tbsp	2 tbsp
Egg	1	1
Brandy/black rum	4 tbsp	4 tbsp
Orange juice	¾ pint	425 ml
Sugar (for syrup)	8 oz	225 g
Almond essence	1–2 tsp	1–2 tsp

If you are making the pasta dough specially, add a drop or two of almond essence. This half recipe will make two trays of ravioli, that is 72; but you can make larger ones without a tray, make the pasta into triangles, into cappelletti or whatever takes your fancy. Once you have made the pasta and rolled it out, cover with a barely damp cloth and prepare the filling.

Mix the coconut, sugar, egg and brandy or rum together and distribute as you would any other pasta filling. Shape your pasta according to the day's whim, and cook in a lot of boiling water just until they float to the top.

Meanwhile heat the orange juice and dissolve the sugar in it and add the almond essence, aiming for a bewitching blend of the two flavours rather than a dominance of one over the other.

Arrange the cooked pasta evenly in a flat dish with sides to it and pour in the hot syrup. Gently toss the pasta to ensure none sticks to another and make sure all are under the liquid. Leave to cool then refrigerate for at least 4 hours. The orange–almond syrup penetrates the pasta and all the flavours blend to make something quite new, with the sudden texture and flavour of the coconut a terrific surprise. Rather stunning by itself, but magical when combined with other puddings. I've served coconut pasta with chocolate ice cream, mixed into a fruit salad, with mango purée and topped with toasted coconut and almonds.

Mocha Mud Pudding

Serves 4–6		
Base		
Flour	4 oz	125 g
Sugar	4 oz	125 g
Baking powder	2 tsp	2 tsp
Salt	½ tsp	½ tsp
Cocoa powder	1 tbsp	1 tbsp
Butter	2 tbsp	2 tbsp
Milk	¼ pint	150 ml
Vanilla essence	1 tsp	1 tsp

Topping/sauce

Sugar, white	4 oz	125 g
Sugar, demerara	4 oz	125 g
Cocoa powder	4 tbsp	4 tbsp
Coffee powder	1 tbsp	1 tbsp
Milk (or water)	¾ pint	425 ml

Preheat the oven to gas mark 4/350°F/180°C. Sift together the dry ingredients of the base. Gently melt the butter in the milk and add the vanilla essence. Beat into the dry ingredients and turn into a *deep* baking dish or oven proof bowl.

Mix together the four dry ingredients of the topping★ and sprinkle over the base. Pour the milk or water over that – it will look awful but trust me. Put the lot into the oven and bake for a good hour. If the top appears to burn, reduce the temperature somewhat. What happens? Miraculously the mud mixture on the top disappears, to emerge underneath a rich sponge pudding as a thick, unbelievably rich sauce. Children like to make this as they can't believe they are allowed to make something so messy; adults love to eat it as it is perhaps the richest and most wicked pudding I know. Few will resist the offer of cream to accompany it.

★ For real chocolate fans, use only brown sugar for the topping and 5 tablespoons of cocoa instead of the cocoa/coffee mixture. This is true chocolate fudge flavour – and won't you know it!

Hot Jaffa Mousse-Soufflé

Serves 6 very richly		
Dark, sweet chocolate	6 oz	175 g
Unsalted butter	4 oz	125 g
Eggs, separated	6	6

Orange rind, grated	6 tsp	6 tsp
Orange juice	6 tbsp	6 tbsp
Sponge fingers	20–22	20–22

Choose a straight-sided soufflé dish of 2½ pint (1.5 litre) capacity and butter well. Cut off the ends of the sponge fingers so they stand with their rounded tops just below the edge of the bowl, sugar side out. The off-cut bits and pieces can be crumbled and spread over the base.

Gently melt the chocolate and butter together and pour into a large bowl; beat in the egg yolks. Grate the orange rind into a small bowl then squeeze the juice into this – thus you gather the zest and oil otherwise lost. Whisk these into the chocolate mixture.

Beat the egg whites until stiff but not dry and fold into the chocolate sauce. There is no need to worry about the odd white streak for that will disappear. Ladle the soufflé into the bowl, then put into a pre-heated oven at gas mark 5/375°F/190°C for 30 minutes. This will give you a nicely risen soufflé with a runny middle – *baveuse* is the smart name for it.

To serve, first cut through the top and serve the crust onto each plate. Then gently portion out the rest of the bowl's contents.

This extraordinarily delicious pudding rises well but still has the rather heavier texture of a mousse rather than the eggy lightness you expect from a soufflé. It really needs the accompaniment of something cool and sharp. Some orange slices, perhaps, some excellent pear or chilled lychees, some raspberries or sliced kiwi fruit in lime juice.

Amazingly this mixture can also be put, uncooked, into small pots and served chilled as a mousse, and jolly good it is too. You don't have to include the sponge fingers in the hot version, but it is far showier if you do.

Spiced Orange-Tea Cake, with Tea Glaze

Serves 8–10

Ceylon tea or tea bags	1 oz	25 g
Milk	½ pint	275 ml
Butter	8 oz	225 g
Sugar	14 oz	400 g
Eggs	4	4
Plain flour	12 oz	350 g
Baking powder	3 tsp	3 tsp
Cinnamon, ground	2 tsp	2 tsp
Allspice, ground	2 tsp	2 tsp
Ginger, ground	1 tsp	1 tsp
Orange, grated rind	1	1

Boil the milk and pour over the tea or tea bags, leave 3–5 minutes, drain well and make the liquid back up to ½ pint or 275 ml with extra milk. Let cool. Preheat oven to gas mark 4/350°F/180°C.

Cream the butter and sugar together really well then beat in the eggs one by one. Sift together the flour, baking powder and ground spices and stir in without overbeating. Mix in the grated orange rind (choose a big orange) then stir in the strong, milk tea mixture. Pour gently into a buttered and floured 8″ (20 cm) square baking tin. Bake 60 minutes – perhaps more depending on your flour and oven.

Immediately you take the cake from the oven prick the top thoroughly with a skewer or fork. Then make the following syrup. Meanwhile cool the cake for 10 minutes. Then remove it and stand it on a rack over a large dish.

Tea Glaze		
Ceylon tea bags	4	4
Orange juice	8 fl. oz	225 ml

Cinnamon, ground	1 tsp	1 tsp
Allspice, ground	1 tsp	1 tsp
Sugar, white	6 oz	175 g

Boil the orange juice and pour over the tea bags, let brew 3 minutes, drain; stir in the sugar and spices. Spoon the syrup over the cake until all is absorbed. Cool then – ideally – keep in a tin for 2 days before it is cut . . . if you can. A really exciting cake this, perhaps the best I have ever put together – and its fascinating flavour and moist texture are a guaranteed success for you.

Real Apple Strudel

10–12 servings		
Strudel pastry (page 70)	1 recipe	1 recipe
Butter, melted	4 oz	125 g
Butter	2 oz	50 g
White breadcrumbs, fresh	2 oz	50 g
Sugar	4 oz	125 g
Mixed spice	3 tsp	3 tsp
Small orange	1	1
Apples, cooking	1½ lb	750 g

Once you have wrought the strudel pastry into sub-mission, and trimmed it to about 18″ × 24″ (45 cm × 61 cm) cut off the edges and paint liberally with melted butter; keep the left-over butter warm.

Melt another 2 oz (50 g) butter in a pan and fry the breadcrumbs until a golden brown. Add the spices, being heavy- rather than light-handed, the sugar and the grated rind of the orange. Stir well and take off the heat. Squeeze the orange's juice into a bowl. Cut the apples into quarters; core, peel and slice them thickly into the orange juice.

Sprinkle the spiced breadcrumbs over the pastry, leaving a border along the two short sides and only going two thirds of the way down the pastry overall, which leaves a good wrap-around for the finished strudel. Spread the apple over the crumbs, keeping it away from the uncrumbed portion and making a good solid line at the opposite edge, which will give a solid middle to the strudel. Dribble the remaining melted butter overall.

Fold in the two short sides then tip the floured cloth to roll up the strudel evenly and on to a baking tray. Turn in the ends so it fits nicely. Bake 50 minutes in a preheated oven at gas mark 4/350°F/180°C. As buttery-syrup escapes, spoon it back over the pastry as it will caramelise to make an attractive, self-decoration. Serve warm or cold with cream. If you want to present it even more prettily, strew a little icing sugar over the top, but do not hide the cascades of caramel.

Pitcairn Cheese & Pineapple Strudel

12 servings

Strudel pastry (page 70)	1 recipe	1 recipe
Melted butter	4 oz	125 g
Curd or cream cheese	1½ lb	750 g
Eggs	3	3
Sugar	4 oz	125 g
Vanilla essence	1 tsp	1 tsp
Pineapple, drained	12 oz	350 g
Raisins or sultanas	2 oz	50 g
Breadcrumbs, dry white	1 oz	25 g
Cinnamon, ground	1–2 tsp	1–2 tsp

Roll, pull, stretch and curse the strudel pastry on a floured sheet or tablecloth until it surrenders up an oblong about 18″ × 24″ (45 cm × 61 cm) – more or less. Trim away the thicker border and paint the remaining paper-thin pastry with melted butter.

Beat together the cheese, eggs, sugar and vanilla. The

pineapple should be cut into small pieces, but some drained crushed pineapple will be almost as good. Mix in the raisins or sultanas, then spread the mixture evenly over the pastry, leaving a border down the short sides and leaving about 25% free at the bottom to make a good surround of pastry when the strudel is rolled.

Sprinkle the cheese with breadcrumbs you have flavoured very well with cinnamon. Pour on the rest of the melted butter. Roll the strudel onto a baking tray as explained on page 71 and twist in the corners to make the classic crescent shape. Bake at gas mark 4/350°F/180°C for 50 minutes or until the strudel is a nice golden colour and a knife inserted into the middle comes out clean.

This is nice when it is hot but is immeasurably better when cold as the cheese flavour miraculously re-develops. For presentation's sake, sprinkle the whole strudel with a little icing sugar and cinnamon.

This is named for Pitcairn Island, home of my Bounty-descendant relatives, where they grow the world's best pineapples – so use fresh pineapple if you possibly can.

SOME BASICS...

Pasta dough

There's absolutely nothing to be frightened about in making pasta. In its most ordinary state, it is simply strong, white flour (bread flour) plus water, but as most of us can now afford to buy eggs, pasta made with eggs is more common these days, which is just as well for it is also more delicious. As with the two pastries which follow, it really is not worthwhile making pasta unless you get bread flour, usually sold as strong white flour. This has a higher quantity of gluten, the protein which becomes elastic to make the bubbles in bread, and which allows you to roll pasta dough so thinly.

The following recipe will make 10–12 oz (275–350 g) of pasta which is 2 reasonable servings of noodles, but rather more servings of stuffed pastas such as ravioli and cappelletti, instructions for which follow.

Pasta dough		
Strong white (bread) flour	8 oz	225 g
Egg	1	1
Olive oil	2 tsp	2 tsp
Water	as required	

Mound the flour in a bowl, create a well, and drop the egg and oil into this. Work these in to the flour and start to add water until you have a soft, dough which you can knead easily. It should not stick to your hands in any way. Knead it for at least 5 minutes, and if you have a good rhythm and nothing else to do, continue for another 5 minutes. Cover the dough with a slightly damp cloth and leave to relax for an hour whilst you do the same.

Now you must roll this dough very thinly indeed – or as thin as you care to, according to the pasta type you are eventually going to make. It can be anything from

⅛" (3 mm) to almost transparent, according to your preference. It is simpler to use one of the pasta-rolling machines, of course. Once rolled, leave the pasta to dry slightly before cutting and shaping.

Here are some instructions to make some of the basic pasta shapes and types.

Noodles

There are two ways to make noodles, which can also be called, fettucine or tagliatelli. You can cut the dry-surfaced pasta into sheets about 4–6" (10–15 cm) wide and as long as you can manage. Then you lay them upon one another and cut them across or lengthwise to make the size and length you wish. A light tossing with the fingers will separate them. Alternatively, flour the sheet well and roll it up quite tightly then cut through at equally individual intervals. Each snail of pasta will unfold during cooking to make a nice long noodle. These can be stored moist by being wrapped in cling film.

Ravioli

To make the best known of the *pasta ripieni*, or stuffed pasta, you need thin sheets of pasta which can then be treated in a number of ways. Simplest is to have two equally sized sheets, to dot filling equally and geometrically on one of them, to cover this with the other sheet, to press the spaces between the two firmly and then to cut them into squares with a special cutter, which is serrated and gives the classic frilled ravioli edge. Naturally you can simply cut them with a knife and call them something else. Or call them 'straight-edged ravioli'.

Or you can buy one of the several varieties of trays which make the construction of ravioli a great deal simpler. When you use these, be certain you put no more filling into the hollows than will lie flat in those spaces or you will have problems of squashing and squishing.

There are also some semi-automatic and machine-driven manufacturers of ravioli, but these are far beyond the scope of anyone other than ravioli maniacs or restaurateurs.

Cappelletti

These are almost the same as tortellini, which are supposed to look like the belly-button of a particularly lovely Italian girl.

You cut your pasta into 2″ (5 cm) squares and dot each with an appropriate stuffing. Fold one corner over the stuffing but do not take it so far that it folds the dough in half. Fold over once again, still leaving a small tail free. Flatten the two arms on either side, then twist them around a suitable finger and join them together. The finished effect should look like a head scarf with no head in it.

If you want to make belly-buttons instead, then you must twist the arms around one another slightly before you join them together.

Strudel Pastry

Unlike the next pastry, strudel needs little or no introduction and ready-made strudel leaves have always been available *somewhere* if you looked hard enough. But making your own is just about the most satisfying thing I know (except – see the piece about eating a mango!) and provided you allow time it is tremendous fun. In fact like many enjoyable pastimes it is even better if you do it with someone else. You can, though, start by yourself . . .

Strudel pastry		
Strong white (bread) flour	8 oz	225 g
Egg	1	1
Oil	1 tbsp	1 tbsp
Salt	pinch	pinch
Water	4 tbsp	4 tbsp

Put the flour onto a board or into a large bowl, make a well in the middle, and add the egg, oil and salt. Slowly knead in the water until you have a smooth dough, and then knead that until the surface is covered with tiny blisters. This will not happen unless you knead properly and with spirit. Then cover with a very slightly dampened cloth and let recover for an hour. Now comes the good bit. And the messy bit.

Clear a table top and cover this with a clean cloth or sheet. Cover with flour and dump the pastry in the centre. Start rolling the pastry and when it is about ½" (1–2 cm) thick leave the rolling pin and start stretching the pastry. There are many ways to do this but basically it works better if one hand is under the pastry and one is on the top. If you have no assistance you will have to weight the opposite side of the pastry at the start or you will simply pull the wretched stuff from one side of the table to the other.

With perseverance and an amount of walking around the table, you will find the pastry starts both to stretch and to stay stretched. As it gets more transparent, you will easily be able to spot the thicker bits and to tease these into submission, perhaps by stroking underneath with outstretched and stiffened fingertips. Try to stretch the border as well, and do not worry if you find holes appearing here and there as these will generally disappear when you roll up the strudel you intend to make. Once you are certain you can stretch the pastry no more, trim off the thick, edge pieces and make the pastry more or less even in shape – a sort of oblong or a sort of oval is best.

If you want to rest or to gloat, paint the whole thing with melted butter first, then cover with a damp cloth. Otherwise go ahead with spreading the filling on the dough, leaving a border on each side (for folding in) and leaving between 25% and 30% free for filling so the final strudel will have a good wrap around of several layers of free, unfilled pastry, which will keep it in shape and give the added attraction of several layers of crispness.

To roll the strudel onto a baking tray, first fold the sheet or cloth back underneath itself until level with the unfilled edge of the strudel. Tuck the baking tray under this folded edge. Now go to the opposite side of the table. Turn in the edge of the strudel by hand to make one roll right along its length then fold in the sides. Complete the rolling by tipping up the cloth, and continue doing this until the completely rolled strudel rolls on to the baking tray; this is another time when it helps to have someone there to help steady the baking tray. There . . . that wasn't so bad, was it?

Phyllo pastry

Sometimes you will see this called *filo* but it is still the paper-thin pastry of Greece and much of the Middle East. It is increasingly available throughout the country, usually frozen, and it is so useful that you should always buy some to keep in your own freezer.

Many of you have probably eaten it without knowing what it was called – usually in the famous greek pastry called baklava, dripping with honey and stuffed with nuts. But it is equally used in all sorts of savoury ways, sometimes wrapped around cheese or spinach and baked, sometimes deep-fried, sometimes used on enormous pies of lamb or chicken.

During my travels I have come across many recipes for making it, but none is so worthwhile as this version. Because you layer it with butter and also roll it very thinly, every sheet is actually three much thinner sheets, each thinner than you could possibly hope to roll independently. The recipe came from a town called Katerini, near Thessalonika in the north east of Greece. It is almost on the slopes of Mt Olympus, so perhaps it has some claim truly to be one of the foods of the Gods?

Phyllo pastry		
makes approx 1½ lb–750 g		
Strong white (bread) flour	1 lb	450 g
Salt	1 tsp	1 tsp
Olive oil	4 tbsp	4 tbsp

Egg	1	1
Vinegar	1 tsp	1 tsp
Water	6 fl. oz	175 ml
Softened butter	4–6 oz	125–175 g

Put the flour into a bowl or onto a clean surface and make a well in the centre, into which put the salt, olive oil, egg and vinegar. Mush these into some of the flour then start kneading in the water until you have a smooth dough that does not stick to your hands. The amount given above is only approximate, of course.

Cover the dough with a slightly damp cloth and leave it to rest for 1 hour in a cool place, which allows it fully to develop its elasticity.

Then divide the dough into 18 pieces of even size and flatten them slightly. Smear 12 of them evenly with softish butter. Then make 6 piles by putting two buttered pieces on top of one another, butter side up, and topping with an unbuttered piece. You will thus have three layers of dough separated by two layers of butter.

Take one pile and start to roll it out, sealing the edges if the butter spurts out too dramatically. Use plenty of flour and when the pastry sheet becomes unwieldy, cut it in half and continue to carefully roll the two pieces separately.

No matter how well you have done, the pastry can *always* be thinner! I find it better to use something as thin as a broom handle rather than the normal rolling pin. To get really excellent results, roll the pastry around the pin and keep rolling, but ensure both sides are particularly well floured or it will all stick together and make you fearfully angry.

Once you have rolled the sheets as much as possible, store them under a dampened cloth, in which state they will last for some time while you have a nice cup of tea and a sit down and generally calm down. Funny to think Greek and Turkish and Arabic women do this every day isn't it?

Making your Praline

Put 6 oz (170 g) of hazelnuts or of unblanched almonds into a heavy-bottomed saucepan together with 6 oz (170 g) of caster sugar. Set over a low heat and leave until colouring very slightly at the edges. Stir with a wooden spoon until the nuts are toasted and the sugar is both clear of grains and a delicious golden brown. Pour on to a cold, lightly oiled metal baking sheet or sheet of baking foil. When cold, break up and grind into a coarse powder and store in an airtight container. Use sprinkled on puddings and on fruit or to flavour creams and icings.

Painting your Pastry

If you've ever heard of the great Coronation banquets once served in Westminster Hall, you'll know that grand medieval food was always highly-coloured and decorated brightly with natural colours. Pastry was red, yellow, green, blue – even gilded with gold and silver leaf. The fun and excitement of richly decorated and coloured pastry doesn't need an army of experts in your kitchen or a crock of gold; and it will be far more rewarding than you can imagine.

When you have put the top on your pastry pie, mark out a pattern, name, or design, with the tip of a knife or with a long fingernail. Using watercolour brushes (or a pastry brush if you are being bold) fill in the pattern using undiluted food colours. Don't have too much on the brush at once for the colour will easily run over the smooth pastry. Let the pastry rest awhile until you can see the colour has been absorbed and the surface has dried. Light colours may benefit from an extra coating.

Once the colour is quite dry, paint over with a glaze of beaten egg yolk; but if it is a big pie that will bake for a long time, wait until later to glaze or it will bake such a deep brown that your colouring will be obscured.

Some ideas? Well, if you make roses or flowers for decoration, paint them and their leaves, but leave the rest of the pastry plain. Paint on the birthdate and name of the child in his favourite colours. Stripe millefeuille pastries with bright red if you are filling them with strawberries and cream, paint a big green apple on an apple pie, or decorate abstractly. A simple criss-cross of bright green on, say, a chicken and leek pie, is very effective, perhaps more so than a complicated pattern. Like so many things to do with food, start simply and progress from there.

Butterflying a Leg of Lamb

Butterflied lamb (or pork or veal for that matter) is the boned and flattened flesh of the leg. It may take some time to get right, but it saves enormous hassle and effort when it comes to serving. Even if your butterflied lamb doesn't look like a butterfly it will cook beautifully and allow you to carve and serve 4–6 people in a fraction of the time it takes to portion out lamb still on the bone.

Depending on how high the leg has been cut from the carcass, you may first have to take out a small joint bone at the top end. There is no easy way to explain this or to do it. You must simply use a small very sharp, pointed knife and slowly excise the bone by removing the flesh. Feel ahead with your finger so you know where to make the next cut. Once exposed, this complicated bone can be severed from the main bone by inserting the knife point into the actual joint and severing the connecting tissues.

Now turn the leg on its side with the knuckle facing you and make a deep straight cut from the top to the knuckle. Then cut either side of the shank down as far as the shin muscle extends. Cut right around the bone at the bottom of your cuts thus freeing the shin meat totally. Starting at the end which looks easier to you, cut around the knuckle joint – it is probably easier to stand the leg on its end with the shank uppermost. There are some complicated bone structures to work about, but as long as you always cut towards the bone, you can't go wrong or damage the meat. Just be patient. All of a sudden the knuckle is free and you can scrape the main bone free. Remove it, lay the flesh skin-side down, and gently cut into the thickest cushions of flesh, so the meat lies as flat as possible. If you can remotely recognise the butterfly shape (actually it is more like a bat I reckon) then trim assiduously to dramatise it. If you have made some other shape, either give it another name or ignore it. It will still taste the same as butter-flied lamb.

You can cook your butterflied leg of lamb on a barbe-cue or in a roasting pan or under a grill. This is cooked flat, skin side up. Rub it with a little salt and some herbs and garlic, after cutting a criss-cross pattern through the fat. In an oven, cook it for 15–20 minutes a lb in a medium oven, gas mark 4/350°F/180°C. Because the flesh varies so much in thickness you will always have some pieces more well done than others, which will please difficult guests, and it almost never goes dry for the fat is dripping through the flesh and basting it throughout the entire cooking process.

The greatest advantage of butterflying leg meat is that once you have let the cooked meat rest for 15 minutes, which ensures that the juices stay in the flesh rather than running into the pan when you cut it, the carving is simple, you just cut slices as though it were a loaf of bread. And that means the carver has a decent chance of eating his or her meal hot, too.

Pocketing a Shoulder of Lamb
Taking out the bone of a shoulder of lamb seems fiendishly complicated, but remember, the animal is dead and you really are its master. Use a sharp pointed knife and work steadily, feeling ahead with your fingers all the time.

The shoulder blade is rather 'T' shaped in profile and has a long ridge only just underneath the skin. Be very careful when dealing with that – you'll never run into trouble if your knife is always angled towards the bone. If you happen to pierce the skin, and you plan to stuff the pocket, go ahead. Cobble the hole together with a toothpick which you weave in and out to make a good join.

When you get to the bottom of the shoulder blade you are at the knee. Cut all round this, too – or at least enough to expose the actual joint.

You can leave the shoulder like this. Once roasted and allowed to sit for the mandatory 15 minutes (so that the juices remain in the meat when you carve it) you simply wrap a cloth around your hand and twist and pull that loosened bone. It should come away immediately giving you a shoulder that is very simple to carve.

Otherwise you sever the shoulder blade bone completely and remove it before cooking. Then widen and deepen the pocket, using the exposed bone which remains as your guide to the bottom of the pocket. This can simply be sprinkled with salt and fresh or dried herbs plus garlic (surprised?) or stuffed with vegetable purées.

Boning Small Fish
The bones of small fish put many a person off eating their flesh – but what delights they miss. There is a simple way of removing most if not all of these pesky things from the raw fish. It works best of all with the smallest fish of all, sprats, herrings and the like, but trout, increasingly common on our tables is also cursed with fine bones and may be so treated to your advantage, too.

Once the fish have been gutted and rinsed, spread the cavity and rest the fish upon this. Then run your thumb along the backbone, pressing it down towards the surface upon which the fish rests. You feel the flesh giving way beneath the pressure.

Turn the fish over and gently pull the spine free, making a cut with kitchen scissors at head and tail. This will still leave a row of fine bones in the flesh. Thus, if you have only a few fish to handle, better to take some time to do the job with a little more finesse and thoroughness.

Once you have pressured the spine, lie the fish on its

side and run a small sharp-pointed knife underneath the bones that lie on the surface. When these are free, very gently push the flesh away from the spine, which will expose the next row of fine bones. Work very gently along the spine until all are exposed, then run the knife under them, too. Turn the fish over and operate on the other side. Then snip the spine at head and tail and remove. Your fish is almost entirely boned and can be stuffed in any way you like.

Bean Talk

Please don't be frightened of dried beans. The method of cooking them all is exactly the same, only the time varies. Simply, you soak them overnight then cook them in plain water without salt. Once that is done you cook them on with fats and vegetables and flavourings; if you give them their initial cooking with salted water you will almost certainly toughen them.

As well as being the greatest possible excuse for eating lots of fatty bacon and garlic sausages – with extra garlic, some goose or bacon fat and then some onions – beans make an excellent extender for certain casserole types of dish. One of my favourites is to start off a casserole of neck of lamb with an amount of water with red or white wine plus tomatoes, onion, bay leaf and garlic while at the same time cooking in unsalted water some of the flat white butter beans. When they are cooked I add the two together and cook on. The beans absorb the fat of the meat and become even sweeter and more luscious. Such one-pot meals cannot really go wrong and are the ideal winter dish when families are rushing in and out playing football or being delayed by weather and transport problems. Left at a low temperature they only improve; if they dry a little, add more water.

Cooked beans make ideal bases for additions to salads, and as with potato salads, it is important to flavour them with vinaigrette whilst they are still warm. Red kidney beans with green pepper cut into small pieces is a great favourite.

If you want beans simply as an accompanying vegetable to a rich stew but don't want them dry, do what the Mexicans do. Take about 20% of the cooked beans out of the saucepan and cook them on with extra liquid until they are a mush. Then stir those back. Naturally you could do this faster in a food processor or liquidiser.

★ ★ ★

When in doubt about any bean dish there are three questions to ask yourself:
1 Should there be more fat?
2 Should there be some, or more, garlic?
3 Should there be some tomato in the dish?

To Hedgehog a Mango

They say the only way really to enjoy a mango is to eat it standing waist deep in the waters of a lagoon, with a friend. Difficult in midwinter in England. Instead, use a sharp, long bladed knife to slice down the side of the mango's large, flat stone to make two 'cheeks'. Carefully cut a criss-cross pattern through the flesh down to the skin then turn the cheek inside out, when the hedgehog shape will appear. Just as a butterflied leg of lamb looks nothing like a butterfly much of the time, this never looks like a hedgehog, but I can't think of something it does look like other than half a World War II hand grenade.

Lime or orange juice makes the simplest accompaniment for the luscious flesh of mango during the day, and in the evening rum can be substituted or also included. If you make a foaming sabayon sauce flavoured with an almond liqueur you will find the contrast of texture and flavour quite exhilarating. Almost as exhilarating as eating a mango with a friend in a waist high lagoon.

Making Tea

The biggest misunderstanding about tea is how long it should be brewed. You can tell just by looking at the leaf – the bigger it is, the longer your tea should brew.

Large leaf teas, usually China teas, should brew 5 to 7 minutes, and some speciality teas with really large leaves may need 9 minutes.
Medium leaves require 3–5 minutes.
Small leaf teas really benefit from a 3 minute brew.

Tea bags. You do not get real tea or flavour by dipping a tea bag in and out of water or by brewing for half a minute in a cup. This instant colour is from a type of tea called a Bright Colouring African and colour does not equal flavour. For the fullest possible flavour from a tea bag, it should brew 2–3 minutes. Of course this makes a very strong brew and thus a properly brewed tea bag can actually stand twice the water you would normally use. This is why tea-bag tea should be made in a tea pot. Otherwise, brew in one cup, then pour half into another and top up with hot water.

Once the tea is brewed properly, it does not stop, but goes on extracting tannin from the leaves and 'stewing' it. To enjoy really fine tea, you should remove the tea bags, or pour the tea off the leaves as soon as it is brewed. I keep another warmed pot for this, as I do not use tea bags. It adds great enjoyment when the second cup tastes the same as the first. And from a health point of view it will help prevent the possibility of actually tanning your stomach lining – which happens if you drink overbrewed tea. What's worse, if you eat cakes and biscuits with stewed tea you are even more likely to tan your stomach and thus perhaps affect your digestion. Lord, is anything safe to eat or drink? I wonder . . .

To make iced tea you break all those rules and soak 4 tea bags per pint of *cold* water for at least 12 hours, which gives you rich colour and flavour without the bitterness of tannin. You can drink this as it is over masses of ice cubes, but it is far nicer to make the cold-brew tea into a tea punch with the addition of citrus juice, pineapple juice (perhaps best of all), spices, sugar, mint and so on.